Parents Acting Badly:

How Institutions and Societies Promote the Alienation of Children from Their Loving Families

FIRST EDITION

Jennifer J. Harman, PhD &
Zeynep Biringen, PhD
The Colorado Parental Alienation Project, LLC

Published by The Colorado Parental Alienation Project, LLC, Fort Collins, CO.

Printed by CreateSpace, an Amazon.com Company

The Colorado Parental Alienation Project, LLC
P.O. Box 271603
Fort Collins, CO 80527

ISBN-13: 978-1519675521

ISBN-10: 1519675526

Contents

Acknowledgements   v

Praise for Parents Acting Badly   xiii

CHAPTERS

Chapter 1   Introduction   1

Chapter 2   What are parental alienating behaviors?   11

Chapter 3   Is research on parental alienation based on good science?   26

Chapter 4   Who are these alienators?   44

Chapter 5   How are alienating behaviors enacted over time?   72

Chapter 6   What kind of relationship do alienated children have with the alienator and how does this affect them?   81

Chapter 7   How does parental alienation impact the targeted parent, family, and community?   103

Chapter 8   How do parental roles, gender, and power contribute to parental alienation?   130

Chapter 9   What other legal and cultural   145

systems enable parental alienation?

Chapter 10   How do perceptions of parenting   165
ability impact the ability for
parents to alienate?

Chapter 11   How can parental alienation be   173
recognized and handled more
effectively?

References   207

ACKNOWLEDGEMENTS

Jennifer J. Harman: There are so many people I want to acknowledge that have been influential in the writing of this book. First and foremost, I want to thank the alienators in my life (there have been a few). The trauma I and those close to me have experienced because of your actions has fueled my intellectual curiosity to better understand your motivations, as well as to understand why we as a society allow these things to happen to our neighbors, friends, and loved ones. I particularly want to thank the most recent alienator in my life-- your direct and indirect stratagems to ruin my professional and personal reputation have provided me with the passion and determination to persist in writing this book. It is unlikely this book will ever compel you to self-reflect and gain awareness about how negatively your children have been impacted by your actions—indeed, I am sure that it will only incite you to continue your campaigns against me and my loved ones. Like most alienators, you will also likely accuse *me* and my partner of the alienating behaviors you, yourself are doing. My only hope is that you can make peace, step back, move on, and let your children have other loving adults in their lives besides just you. I thank all of you for the opportunity to turn my pain and trauma into something that can be of benefit to others.

I also want to thank all of the excellent mentors and colleagues I have been honored to work with during my professional training and career. They have each knowingly and unknowingly contributed to the ways I see the world, which has afforded me the ability to frame this devastating problem using a social psychological lens. I am positive I will leave out many important people, but special thanks to Vita Rabinowitz, Blair Johnson, Felicia Pratto, Jeffrey Fisher, K. Rivet Amico, Lisa Neff, Jeffery Simpson, M'Lou Caring, Winthrop Atkins, Michelle Kaufman, Nancy Levinger, Debra Warner, Vernon Smith, Zinta Byrne, all of my colleagues at the ScienceofRelationships.com (& MERRG) and of course, my co-author, Zeynep Biringen.

My excellent research team of graduate and undergraduate students have also been an immense help in processing and thinking about many of the themes and issues that appear in this book. Special thanks to James McDonald, Carlie Trott, Pearl Outland, Ellen Ratajack, Allyson Kraus, and all others who join us for our monthly happy hour lab meetings. The list of undergrads I would like to thank is too long to outline here, but you know who you are! Your personal stories and drive to help with this project have been an inspiration. This work would not have been possible without you.

To the 82 parents we interviewed for our research project: I want to thank each and every one of you for your stories. I know it was painful and scary to share them with us, particularly to relive traumatic events that will never have resolution. You are all strong and deserving to have your children in your lives, and I am so sorry that our society and institutions have allowed this to happen to you. I hope that this book represents your truth and experiences accurately, and please know that we will continue to explore different dimensions of this problem for many years to come, thanks to your stories.

I also need to thank the wonderful people in my life who have provided me personal support throughout this process. My children and step-children bring me joy each and every day, and I am thankful that despite what the alienators in my life have done so far, our relationships have weathered their actions. You each demonstrate such resilience and capacity for love, and I appreciate your optimism and ability to persevere even when things are emotionally very tough. I love you all. My family has always encouraged me to study and work hard, and they all have been supportive of me during the roughest of personal and professional times. Thank you Mom, Dad, Eric, and Elonn.

Last but not least, I want to thank my soul mate and best friend, Matt Florian. Our beautiful journey together has been hard-earned, and continues to be a target for those who are unhappy with their own lives. Despite this, our love and relationship continues to grow. Your personal experience and insight about parental alienation has opened my eyes to how parental alienation affects those who are targeted, and I have greatly appreciated your feedback and encouragement to get this book done so that it can be of use to help other parents who are living with this problem every day. I love you and thank you for everything.

Zeynep Biringen: The area of parental alienation is very far from my personal experiences, as I have been happily married to the same person for many years. Thank you, Sedat Biringen, for being my secure base throughout most of my life and all of my career as a child psychologist and professor. Your support and our partnership has kept me on track, and has given me the strength to help children and families to also have a secure base in their lives. I have been lucky enough to raise my daughter Erin in a home where both sides of our families have been welcome, excited, and eager to show her the love she deserves. Erin has taught me more than I could have imagined and shown me that love is not only about being emotionally connected but also about being able to let go. She is now 21 years old with a strong, determined, and insightful personality, and communicates in an honest and open way. We don't always agree. However, we both feel secure enough to speak our strong minds! Despite loving circumstances on both sides of our family system, I have personally seen how challenging it is to raise children. I can only begin to imagine how this terrain must be for those who find land mines scattered throughout their journey.

I became interested in the topic of parental alienation because of my deep interest in the topic of emotional availability (and unavailability) of parents to their children *and* children to their parents! I have been training researchers as well as practitioners to judge these qualities for decades, and endorse the idea that the *actual as well as the perceived* nature of relationships can influence an *observed* relationship. As well, any parent-child relationship involves a two-way street.

I firmly believe that some alienation of children happens in many divorcing/divorced families as well as intact families. It is our job as grown and emotionally healthy adults to be reflective about our lives in order to expose our children to peaceful (rather than hostile) relationships or, at the very least, expose them to relationships in which conflicts and hostilities get resolved. Children are the losers (in the short or long run) when they are exposed to or closely involved in the hostilities. They should be allowed the freedom to love and be supported by both parents and to think independently and with nuance (rather than in black/white terms) about these relationships.

The title of our book is "Parents *acting* badly" which suggests that "Parents *can* also act well." There is an element of acting, which suggests that even when parents harbor mutual resentment, they can still act well -- for the sake of the children--and then the children also learn to act well. However, individuals need to experience that "playing nice" can benefit them, and this is where societies and institutions can be invaluable. *Not only should institutions and societies promote child support payments, but should also promote the monitoring of access to the children and not financially reward a parent who limits or blocks access to the children or psychologically alienates the children from a caring parent. It would be innovative to establish an entity to monitor both at the same time.* If a parent would like to have a relationship with his or her children and has not been found guilty of abuse, neglect, or violence, that parent should not "ambiguously" lose the right to be a parent. All in all, it is important to heed psychosocial research, which indicates that young people benefit from having two loving parents, particularly if there has been an adequate relationship prior to the break up.

I'd like to thank the participants of the Affect, Stress, and Prevention Seminar (ASAP) at the University of Colorado School of Medicine, a forum for discussing issues relevant for children, including at times this particular issue. I thank the policy organization Zero to Three and the Academy of Zero to Three Fellows for shaping my thinking on bringing research to action and policy change, particularly for very young children. I thank the many families and legal professionals who have contacted me over the years about being an expert witness or custody evaluator in divorce cases. I have referred them to others, but such interest in the concept of emotional availability and emotional unavailability as it applies to divorcing families, custody, or social service evaluations has helped me to get here and to focus on parental alienation—the ultimate form of emotional *un*availability within a family system. I thank our study families most sincerely for their openness, their reflectiveness about what has happened to them, and their quest to find positive solutions, including contributing their stories to bring awareness to a problem swept under the rug!

I thank Colorado State University for providing the intellectual climate in which new ideas can form and our graduate and honors students investigating this topic: Allyson Kraus, Chelsea Kline, Amy Smith, and Courtney Gaskins. Thank you Jennifer Harman for your dedication and collaboration on the Colorado Parental Alienation Project, so we can bring voice to our participants' disenfranchised grief and trauma, and the issues faced by 22 million others in the U.S., as well as many more across different cultures around the world. How can this be happening in good societies to good parents?

PRAISE FOR PARENTS ACTING BADLY

"I have long held that the growing problem of parental alienation is primarily systemic in nature, its driving force being an adversarial system that forces parents to denigrate each other in an effort to win the custody of one's children. This is an important addition to the growing research on the etiology of alienation, offering a sociocultural perspective through the eyes of the overlooked victims of alienation - disenfranchised parents and their children. In this meticulous analysis, Harman and Biringen expose the legal abuse and systemic victimization of parents who are forcefully removed from their children's lives by means of primary residence judgments. A powerful testimony that speaks to the urgency of needed socio-legal reform for the betterment of children and families."

> **Edward Kruk, PhD,** Associate Professor of Social Work, The University of British Columbia, specialist in child and family policy.

"After interviewing mothers and fathers from around the world, Harman and Biringen provide compelling new answers and solutions to a REAL social problem facing millions of families worldwide – parental alienation. They reframe parental alienation as a social and cultural problem, and help us recognize that we are all responsible for its prevalence and solutions. For anyone who is a member of a family – intact, divorced, or blended – I highly recommend this book!"

Dr. Terri Orbuch, author of *5 Simple Steps to Take Your Marriage From Good to Great,* Professor at Oakland University, Research Professor at University of Michigan, therapist, and The Love Doctor®

"At last, Harman and Biringen have taken a social and cultural lens to better understand this devastating problem that affects millions of families. The examples they provide throughout the book, taken from in-depth interviews with parents from around the world, serve to illustrate the traumatic grief and struggles that I see every day in my practice working with parents who are alienated from their children. The authors provide an excellent analysis of not only the clinical implications of parental alienation on children, but the effects on the parents, extended families, and their entire social networks. Parental alienation isolates children within one part of the family system and does not give children a chance to continue their relationships with the family as a whole. They also provide substantial support for why effective interventions addressing parental alienation need to work closely with social institutions (e.g., judicial systems), and how each and every one of us can do something to fix this problem. The book makes us think twice about whether a parent has abandoned his or her children or if that parent has been locked out of the children's lives after divorce. I strongly recommend this book to anyone who is a parent, knows a parent, or works with parents who are dealing with another who is distancing them from their children."

Kathleen Reay, PhD., Founder and Director of the Family Reflections Reunification Program,

Inc. and the International Institute for Parental
Alienation Studies (IIPAS), Author of *Toxic
Divorce: a Workbook for Alienated Parents*

CHAPTER ONE

INTRODUCTION

Parental alienation is a serious problem of epidemic proportions that has only recently started drawing serious public attention. There are many examples of Hollywood celebrities who have been targeted (e.g., Alec Baldwin) or are victims of it (e.g., Kate and Oliver Hudson). In 2014, the actor Jason Patric won back parental rights of his son after a lower court had taken them away. Because of his experience, and with the support his Hollywood friends (e.g., Keifer Sutherland, Matt Damon, Mel Gibson), he founded *Stand up for Gus,* a charity that provides resources such as legal aid and education for alienated parents.

There has also been an explosion of media attention and organizing efforts related to parental alienation over the last ten years. Meetup.com, a web-based social network service, shows over 66 groups having formed since 2009 related to parental alienation with over 3,500 members. Hundreds of Facebook pages have been founded since 2005 devoted to this topic, with members ("likes") ranging from 55 to nearly 5,000 members worldwide. A recent Google search of the term "parental alienation" has yielded over three quarters of a million links, news stories, books, and videos.

Many video documentaries have been produced and distributed in the U.S. and abroad (e.g., Germany) to bring awareness of parental alienation to the general public. The recent Divorce Corp. documentary (based on the book of the same name) sought to expose family court corruption and bring to the forefront part of this issue that is affecting millions of families worldwide. Since its release in 2014, Divorce Corp. has put out a Call for Action with the intent of forming committees to advocate for family law reform and to organize conferences to educate and develop strategies to effectively change public policies and family laws that exacerbate parental alienation.

Since just 2012, Saskatchewan (Canada) and 11 U.S. states have either held hearings, prepared, or proposed equal parenting bills aimed to equalize parenting time with children and to give the courts recourse to address common alienating behaviors such as interference with child visitation and temporary custody orders. Two recent ballot initiatives promoting equal parenting time have also been proposed in the last few years in North Dakota (defeated twice) and one in Washington State that did not make the ballot in 2015. There is also a gofundme.com initiative underway in Nebraska to raise enough funds to have an equal parenting time measure on an upcoming election ballot in the near future. Unfortunately, nearly all of these initiatives to date have been blocked, vetoed, or defeated at the polls.

Why is this issue such a problem today? Why do so few people know about it or deny its existence? Has it always been a problem and we are only now more aware of it? Why is there such resistance to legislative and judicial reforms to address it? Who is resistant? Is this a problem resting primarily in family courts? With public sentiment?

Deeply held gender beliefs? Books and research papers on this topic so far have provided very clear descriptions of what parental alienating behaviors are, their impact on children and families, and have provided clinical and legal recommendations, but we were still left with the question of **"WHY?"** And why has this problem gotten so bad?

One of us (Dr. Harman) has been the target of severe parental alienation herself. As a researcher of intimate relationships, coping involved trying to understand what was going on in her blended family of five children. She reached out to the other author (Dr. Biringen), a child psychologist focusing on issues of attachment and emotional availability. After several lengthy conversations and a mutual desire to get a better grasp of the problem, the Colorado Parental Alienation Project was born.

Prior to meeting together to form a research plan, we surveyed the literature on the topic. Many of the resources we found about parental alienation have been largely descriptive and drawn from practitioners' clinical or legal caseloads. While these resources are useful to draw attention to the problem, we did not want to write another book filled with long case histories, clinical impressions, and legal recommendations. Such publications are important starting points because the authors have been documenting the existence of this problem based on their professional work in the trenches for the last few decades. Rather, we wanted to build on this knowledge and reframe how we think about it—it is a social and cultural problem, not just a private one

We decided to start from scratch. Abandon all we know. Talk to people who have been the targets of parental alienating behaviors. Hear their stories. Look for commonalities and themes that tie their experiences together. Our hope was that we would confirm what other researchers have found (adding support to the existence of this problem) and also uncover new social and cultural factors that contribute to the problem and have not been explored or clearly articulated yet.

We recruited people from a wide variety of sources because we did not want to interview only parents who belong to parental alienation support and advocacy groups. We started with several social media sites (Facebook, LinkedIn) related to divorce, single parenting, as well as parental alienation. Our recruitment posts contained a brief description of the study, and presented a hyperlink to an on-line survey that gathered general information about the parent who is the target of alienation (who we will call the targeted parent throughout this book), their children, their relationship with the other parent, and different types of alienating behaviors they experienced. We also emailed the organizers of nearly one hundred Meetup.com groups devoted to alimony and court reform, divorce, single parenting, and parental alienation. The organizers shared details of the study with their members who then accessed the link to the survey.

At the end of the survey, we asked whether each respondent would like to be interviewed, and if so, to provide their email address. In all of our years as researchers, neither of us expected to have such a high response rate. Almost every week, we received phone calls and emails from parents all over the world, asking to share their stories. In a span of only 3 months, over 700 people across the entire socioeconomic spectrum completed the on-line survey, and we have interviewed 82 fathers and mothers from around the world (e.g., Australia, Canada, England, India, Turkey, the Netherlands, Trinidad & Tobago, the U.S.) for between 1-2 hours each. This is the largest interview study either of us have ever undertaken, and we believe it to be the largest qualitative study on the topic to date.

The stories that were shared with us were simultaneously inspiring and devastating. They were stories of pain, disenchantment, trauma, and helplessness, as well as optimism and resilience in the face of ongoing trauma perpetrated within the family system. It is important to note that although we did not request it of them, over half of the parents we interviewed independently emailed or offered us court documents, psychological reports, correspondence exchanges, and other materials to corroborate their sides of the stories. These parents were desperate for someone to take their predicament seriously—many felt alone in their experience. One mother we interviewed aptly stated, "when you become an alienated parent, your society alienates you as well." Some parents did not even know of or call their experience parental alienation, and yet their stories were just like all the others we heard. The fact that each story was so similar, no matter who or where the unacquainted participants were from, demonstrates the validity and existence of this global problem.

Each story stayed with us, and at times haunted us for days at a time. We were often left with the feeling that this problem is so big there is nothing that can be done about it. This feeling only fueled our passion to continue. We kept interviewing. When researchers conduct interview research like this, it typically ends at a point called *saturation*, or when each additional interview does not really add anything new to what has already been learned. Depending on the topic, saturation can occur after a few interviews or after many. In our case, we reached saturation with fathers after about 15 interviews. We continued on anyway, searching for a story that was unique, or different than what others before had shared. Saturation was more difficult to reach with mothers. There were many mothers and step-mothers; no step-fathers. This interesting discrepancy will be discussed later in this book.

Our interviewing team, which was made up of ourselves and three graduate research assistants, met regularly to discuss impressions and commonalities across the different types of relationships we learned about. We have also had a team of over 25 undergraduate students assist with transcribing these interviews, and met monthly with them as well to gather their impressions and perspectives of what they heard. This was a painful and illuminating process. Several students, who themselves had been child victims of parental alienation, could not bear to listen to the stories; they experienced painful flashbacks when they listened to what seemed like their own lives described by others. Others were the half siblings of children being alienated by the other parent, and they struggled with alienation from the parent as well as their half-siblings. These students wanted to understand better why this was happening. The Colorado Parental Alienation Project grew from just an idea to write this book on the problem. We were so inspired by the experiences of the people we interviewed that we have formulated a number of research projects that will be published separately in academic journals.

This book draws from the themes that came out of these interviews. Before we get to addressing the "why" question, we first need to outline what parental alienation is, and what led us to this point. We will share snippets of our interviewees' stories to illustrate the severity and scope of this problem that leaves many targeted parents depressed, traumatized, and at times suicidal.

Although the main purpose of our book is to reframe the parental alienation problem as a social and cultural problem rather than as a private/domestic one, we also wanted to illustrate in greater detail what the experience of the targeted parent looks like. In doing so, we were initially going to present examples of mild, moderate, and severe cases. But how does one define severity? Is it in terms of how it impacts the child or the targeted parent, or both? Is it determined by severity of the derogation of the targeted parent? Or is it the degree and length of time that there is minimized or restricted contact between the children and the targeted parent? Is it related to the amount of legal involvement the families have had to endure? Illustrating these different types of severity can be a very complex process.

For simplicity's sake and due to the limited space available in a book of this type, we decided to make available on our book's website (parentsactingbadly.com) two detailed illustrations about how alienation has affected both a targeted father and mother. By condensing the stories that were shared with us, we try to give voice to the victims in a way that does not single out specific parents that we interviewed, but rather give their painful experiences a voice and show that there are many others who share their plight. These stories also show that while some elements of the stories may seem strange or extreme, they are *not* unique to particular families. They are experiences that *many* targeted parents shared with us. We encourage readers to explore these expanded stories if they are interested in learning more about what the parental alienation process looks like over time.

Solutions so far have not made a dent in decreasing the prevalence of parental alienation: family court reform measures, equal parenting bills, and ballot initiatives are regularly defeated or tabled due to lack of support, research evidence, or special interest group intervention. Yet, many professionals working with children and families inaccurately believe that courts are aware of or adequately take this problem into account when working to allocate and monitor parenting time. Our hope with this book is to not only reframe the very real problem of parental alienation, but to suggest more effective solutions. Parental alienation is the domestic violence of our time; although many people deny its existence, we need to address the "elephant in the room." We need better theories to explain it. Here is a start.

CHAPTER TWO

WHAT ARE PARENTAL ALIENATING

BEHAVIORS?

Many police, mental health, and legal professionals today deny the existence of parental alienation, and many more have no idea what it even is. Sadly, this lack of awareness and denial has resulted in the suffering of millions of children and families around the world, with little hope for an effective solution to be developed or implemented. Although there have been a number of practitioners, policy makers, and advocacy groups who have attempted interventions to address this problem, they have been met with considerable resistance. We will address this resistance issue later in this book, but first we need to provide an overview of what parental alienating behaviors actually are.

Parental alienating behaviors are a set of behaviors that one parent does (usually intentionally) with the intent to distance and damage a child's relationship with the other parent. There are many situations in which a child's negative reactions or feelings towards a parent are justified, such as in cases where the parent has been abusive or neglectful; this is considered *estrangement*. Parental alienating behaviors are different than estrangement in that they are *unjustified* and *disproportionate* to what the other parent may or may not have done.[1] In other words, while a child may be estranged from a parent due to legitimate shortcomings in their abilities to be a parent, the alienating parent will exaggerate these, or make them seem worse than what the parent actually did in order to turn a child against them. Alienating behaviors, whether they are obvious or subtle, promote an unhealthy (or severed) relationship with the targeted parent. For example, a parent may have shortcomings due to struggles with depression, which can make a child feel estranged from them. An alienating parent would then exaggerate the impact this depression has had on the child, distancing the child further from the targeted parent.

Despite what many believe about parental alienation, this is not typically a bidirectional process: it is not something that results from negative interactions between the targeted parent and the child, nor is it something that is a result of two parents in a high conflict divorce or separation doing it to each other. While there are sometimes cases of two parents alienating their children at the same time, it is usually just one parent turning on the other after the relationship ends. With the support of their social networks, legal advice, and other social and cultural institutions, the alienating parent begins an unrelenting campaign of persecution and harassment of the targeted parent, using children as pawns in this sick "game." We believe parental alienating behaviors fall on a spectrum (mild to severe) and may exist even before the end of the marriage.

Historical origins of the "parental alienation" term

While parental alienation has been evidenced in the courts dating back to the 19th century, it was in 1976 that clinicians Judith Wallerstein and Joan Kelly[2] began writing about this phenomenon in high-conflict divorcing or divorced families. They noted that children in these families had distanced themselves from one of the parents and refused to visit them. Although they did not use the term parental alienation to describe what they were observing, they described the child's rejection behavior as "pathological alignment." They also noticed that many vulnerable children formed what they called an "unholy alliance" with one parent who often had personality problems; many times this alliance entailed joining forces against the other parent. Wallerstein and Kelly noted that these alliances did not appear to be long lasting; within two years of divorce, most of the children they worked with were no longer rejecting a parent. Given what we have learned since this seminal study was published, these families represent a mild form of parental alienation that is fairly easy to repair.

It was not until 1985 that the term *Parental Alienation Syndrome* (PAS) was first coined based on the clinical experiences of Dr. Richard Gardner.[3] Dr. Gardner noticed that children whose parents were embroiled in high conflict custody disputes often experienced psychiatric problems. Importantly, these issues were not reported as occurring during the marriage or after divorce when there was low conflict between the ex-spouses. Gardner described a family dynamic of a vengeful parent (typically the mother) who engages in behaviors like badmouthing the other parent in order to damage the relationship between a child from the non-custodial parent (usually the father). The child (or children) eventually comes to believe the parent's overt badmouthing of the other parent as fact, and then starts to distance themselves from the targeted parent. Because *these distancing tactics are maintained over a long period of time*, Gardner likened these behaviors to propaganda, programming, or brainwashing of the child or children in the family. In other words, Gardner's perspective was that PAS occurs when a pathological primary caregiver sabotages the relationship between the child and the non-custodial parent.

Gardner was one of the first clinicians to outline parental alienation behaviors that were indicative of PAS, and these included, in Gardner's words:

> "1. a campaign of denigration of the targeted parent;
>
> 2. weak, frivolous, and absurd rationalizations for the deprecation;
>
> 3. lack of ambivalence in the child;
>
> 4. the "independent thinker" phenomenon;
>
> 5. reflexive support of the alienating parent in the parental conflict;
>
> 6. absence of guilt over cruelty to and/or exploitation of the targeted parent by the alienating parent;
>
> 7. presence of borrowed scenarios (e.g., events that happened to someone else);
>
> 8. spread of animosity to the extended family of the alienated parent." (p.1)[3]

In other words, PAS is the result of a child feeling hostility towards the targeted parent when the cause of the hostility is unjustified. Hostility towards a parent when it *is* justified (estrangement) is *not* considered PAS. Based on his clinical experience with clients, Gardner's presumption that fathers are more often the targets of parental alienation than mothers appears to have been influenced by his clinical experiences and his own beliefs rather than drawn from empirically-based research conducted with the general population.

Why do many people today deny the existence of PAS? Gardner believed and vehemently asserted that most claims of abuse made by alienating parents during custody battles were fabricated. One reason for his opinion was that he often witnessed children being coerced by the alienating parent into corroborating false sexual abuse allegations against the targeted parent. These allegations often occurred during or right after a custody dispute when the alienating parent was trying to get sole custody or more parenting time with the children. Indeed, we heard of alienating parents using many false allegations in our interviews in an attempt to get custody of their children.

Unfortunately, Gardner's coining and use of the PAS term created substantial unease among clinicians, legal professionals, and researchers about recognizing PAS as a legitimate phenomenon. While the tactics and behaviors presented by him are well documented by other researchers studying PAS and have been evident in our own interviews with parents, *his lack of objectivity and critical thinking about the topic definitely has had a negative effect on the scientific advancement of this important area.* Many critics have tried to discredit Gardner's work by falsely claiming he never published peer-reviewed articles (despite having published over 130, nineteen on the topic of parental alienation) and that he only self-published, despite having over half a dozen major publishers of his books, including Prentice-Hall and Doubleday.[4]

PAS and the Diagnostic and Statistical Manual-5

In 2008 and 2010, William Bernet proposed that Parental Alienation Syndrome (PAS) be considered a mental disorder of the child and that it should be included in the 5th edition of the Diagnostic and Statistical Manual (DSM), which is used by mental health professionals to diagnose and treat their patients.[5] Bernet believed that a child with PAS has a false belief that one parent has abandoned and does not love him or her, is a bad parent, or did bad things in the relationship. Like Gardner, he also emphasized that this phenomenon would not be called PAS if the targeted parent was in fact a bad parent. He argued that what makes PAS a disorder is that there is not support for accusations of sexual or physical abuse and/or neglect by the alienated parent, and yet the child believes in and/or colludes in the malevolent rejection of the targeted parent. Unfortunately, family courts often *assume* domestic violence, physical abuse, sexual abuse, and/or neglect without any evidence, a shortcoming we will cover in a later chapter.

Despite their eloquent description of PAS that was submitted to the DSM-5 Taskforce,[6] Bernet and colleagues' proposal was rejected for several reasons. First, the taskforce decided that a PAS diagnosis could not fully describe all the problems that result from the alienating behaviors of a parent. Second, there are already diagnostic codes for parent-child relationship problems that include child abuse, so PAS could already be reflected in those codes. In fact, *the newest edition of the DSM does mention parental alienating behaviors as a type of abuse.* The third reason is that DSM diagnoses are for individual disorders. If an adult is diagnosed with borderline personality disorder because of how he or she relates to others, the disorder itself rests within the individual. PAS is the result of a parent's behavior and not something internally wrong with a child. Additionally, the DSM is not a compendium of the causes of mental disorders. Thus, a child might be diagnosed with conduct or oppositional defiant disorder using a DSM code, but the reason(s) a child has developed these disorders are not included in the DSM.

Our perspective on this issue is that parental alienation is a set of behaviors that have a very negative impact on children and the entire family dynamic. It is *emotionally abusive* and affects how children perceive past, current, and future relationships. We also agree with Anna Lavadera and colleagues, who argue that parental alienation is a form of psychological harassment,[7] designed as a way for a parent to target the other parent by using the children as weapons; they are a means to an end. Although children who have been alienated from a parent struggle with many cognitive and emotional problems, these problems are outcomes of a parent's behaviors. Therefore, rather than push to have PAS be considered a psychological disorder, we believe it is more productive to focus on the individual factors of the parent who is doing the alienating, such as whether there are existing mood or personality disorders (e.g., borderline personality disorder), that contribute to their putting their own needs and desire for revenge ahead of their children's mental and emotional well-being. It is also important to consider how our social and legal institutions sanction and even promote these behaviors, which we will address later in this book.

New terminologies, same phenomena

Despite the controversy around using the PAS term, clinicians and researchers have continued to publish and report on this issue using different terminologies.

Janet Johnston and her colleagues[8] have preferred the term *Alienated Child* (AC), focusing their attention on how a child is affected by the alienating behaviors of a parent. These researchers have proposed many explanations for why a child would reject and be hostile towards the alienated parent, including the history of that relationship, their own vulnerability during times of stress, and whether the targeted parent is passive and gives in to the domination of the other parent. Importantly, these researchers did not blame the primary caregiver (or one parent) entirely for this unhealthy dynamic.

Johnston and her colleagues also proposed that alienating dynamics operate along a continuum. On one end of this continuum, a child enjoys a positive relationship with both parents. On the other end, a child rejects a parent with no documented violence, abuse, or neglect. These children are potentially responding to complex and frightening family dynamics that may be distorting their views of themselves and the other parent. Children and adolescents on this end of the spectrum reject and are hostile towards the targeted parent *with little to no ambivalence or guilt*; they have fully adopted the alienating parent's negative portrayal as their own.

In between these two extremes are mild to moderate forms of alienating. Near the positive end of the continuum, a child has a close affinity with one parent, but still likes to see the other. There is also the possibility that the child's affinity might change over time. More moderate positions on the continuum are characterized by allied children who have a consistent preference for one parent over the other, but do not fully reject the targeted parent, or they persistently reject a parent and have legitimate reasons to feel distant (e.g., the parent has been violent). When there are legitimate reasons for rejection, then other professionals have considered this position on the continuum estrangement rather than alienation.

In support of their perspective, Johnston conducted a study examining factors that predicted why 215 children rejected a parent after divorce.[9] While there were many limitations of the study (which Johnston acknowledges), there were some interesting conclusions. First, the typical child had a father who was apparently deficient in parenting skills, did not understand the child well, or could not communicate well with them. This lack of connection may be due to having little or poor quality contact with the child. Second, the child's relationship with the mother *appeared* to be warmer and more supportive than with the father; however, in reality, the mother had unmet emotional or dependency needs that were being put upon the child. This behavior then resulted in a co-dependency between the child and the mother that undermined and sabotaged the relationship with the father.

Johnston also found that older children are more vulnerable to this co-dependency then younger children due to their cognitive and emotional capacity to be like a peer to the alienating parent. Children who are overly-connected or experience anxiety about separation with the alienating parent also align closely with them. Note in these descriptions, as well as the findings from our own research, that children who reject their parents are not balanced and emotionally healthy; their apparent close attachment to the alienating parent is, by scientific assessments of attachment, considered insecure or dependent (another topic we will take up later in this book).

In summary, Johnston's perspective is that the problematic parenting and emotional well-being of both parents creates an alienated child, and these arise from deficits in parents' parenting skills. She also suggests that women are more easily able to distance the children from the father than vice versa, perhaps because women have greater access to the children (e.g., more custody) or because they are closer to them emotionally.

Douglas Darnall has used the term *Parental Alienation* (PA) in his research, however his emphasis has been on the process, rather than the outcome of PA on a child.[10] This view is different than the definitions reviewed so far, in that a parent can begin a process of alienating the child but it is unlikely that each and every child will succumb to their overt or covert propaganda. In other words, children are not passive pawns in this dynamic. It is possible that a child may not be aware of the alienating tactics and will continue to seek out visitation with the other parent, or that at one point, perhaps the tipping point, the child moves to the targeted parent's side. Becoming alienated is just that: a process— and even apparently subtle, unintentional, harmless comments that deprecate a parent in front of a child may set into motion this process. Over time, the child begins to see the targeted parent as having little control and being less worthy of their love, hence their role as a parent in the context of the family system becomes diminished.

Important controversies and manipulations

Parental alienation as a label has been misused by some parents to get their way in court. For example, a father who is a perpetrator of child abuse or intimate partner violence may claim that he is not abusive, but that

the mother is just alienating his children from him.[11]
There are many highly visible cases in the media where
one parent (who in fact was or is abusive, physically or
sexually) is given access to the child(ren) and the child
continues to be abused.[12]   Citing such circumstances,
some abusers have enlisted the help of their attorneys to
get partial or sole custody of the child(ren), using
"parental alienation" as a defense.   When they are
successful, the abusive parent gains access to and isolates
a child in an abusive context, stripping the other parent
(who may be better adjusted) of their role as a protector.
*The frequency with which parental alienation is misused in this way
is uncertain and needs to be discovered.* Unfortunately, many
people use these examples as evidence that parental
alienation is *always* misused, and this opinion outright
dismisses the experiences of parents who *are* legitimately
being alienated from their children. In our work, and that
of many other researchers, most parental alienation
occurs in contexts where both parents were "good-
enough;" not perfect, but not abusive-- there is often no
real proof that there has been any physical or sexual abuse
history.

There is not one type of parent who monopolizes
the role of "alienator."   Mothers, fathers, step-mothers,
step-fathers all can play this hand when scorned.   Being a

target is also not limited to those in the parental role, either. We had many people contact us who were alienated grandparents and extended family members. Many of these individuals had very strong relationships with the children involved, and had even fewer (or no) legal rights than parents to stop the alienation. While these non-parental relationships are not the focus of our book, they are important to consider given that parental alienating behaviors are often modeled and transmitted across generations. The supports children have from other adults in their lives are important buffers against the effects of parental alienation, and when these supports are blocked, the children experience greater suffering.

CHAPTER THREE

IS RESEARCH ON PARENTAL ALIENATION
BASED ON GOOD SCIENCE?

Janet Johnston has argued that there has been little sound empirical research on parental alienation,[1] and this has impacted the acceptability of the term in scientific and clinical communities. For quite some time, Gardner's name was synonymous with the *Parental Alienation Syndrome* (PAS) term and when he fell from grace because of his outspokenness and incredulity about sexual abuse allegations, the term itself also fell into disfavor and stunted research advancement on this topic.

Many eloquent legal scholars and researchers of human development[2,3] have debunked and been critical of parental alienation being a syndrome, and some have even claimed it has been based on "junk" science. In fact, we heard this sentiment quite a lot in our interviews and meetings with law enforcement, legal professionals, and many researchers: they believe that parental alienation is not based on good science, so therefore it must not exist. But what is "good" science? The answer to this question is very important if parental alienation is to ever be considered a legitimate phenomenon.

The scientific method is an approach to answering questions that is conducted by making observations and running experiments in an objective manner. There are three basic types of questions that scientific researchers ask: *descriptive*, *explanatory*, and *predictive*.

Descriptive studies. These studies address questions about the general nature of the problem. How common is it? How frequently do specific behaviors take place? Essentially, this kind of research is meant to answer questions about "What is this?" As we noted earlier, most research on parental alienation to date has been primarily descriptive, which is a necessary first step to begin the documentation of a phenomenon's existence. Indeed, we argue that because of the controversies around whether parental alienation exists at all, researchers have had to spend a considerable amount of time trying to demonstrate its very existence. Therefore, we, and others have argued that research in this area is in its infancy. It is not likely many people today would deny the existence of domestic violence, and much of the early research on that topic was also descriptive because the extent of the problem needed to be documented.

What do our descriptive studies tell us about what parental alienation is? Research *has* documented a wide range of parental alienating behaviors reported by adults targeted by alienation, as well as children across the developmental spectrum. Although many psychologists working with divorced families report increases in the prevalence of parental alienation over the years,[4] there is still debate among professionals about its actual prevalence.

Parental alienation affects mostly divorced families, but it also exists in non-divorced "intact" families. It is also an international problem, with parental alienation groups and organizations existing in countries all over the world. A review of divorce cases in Rome, Italy between 2000 and 2006 resulted in the identification of severe parental alienation occurring in 12% of cases.[5] Only moderate-to-severe cases of parental alienation typically make their way to the courts for intervention, so estimates of prevalence from legal case reviews are likely grossly underestimated. The data do not include families that have milder forms of parental alienation or lack financial resources to seek legal intervention.

Amy Baker reports prevalence of parental alienation at about 25%, based on reports from New York child welfare agency employees,[6] and some researchers estimate the presence of parental alienation is between 2-80% of divorced families.[7] This wide range suggests that there may not be consensus in terms of what people believe parental alienation is or the severity of the problem. For example, 2% prevalence may reflect *very* severe alienation, while 20% may reflect more mild or moderate cases, and 80% may reflect that a substantial majority of children suffer *some* form of relationship distancing from a parent.

William Bernet used a different approach to estimate prevalence: Twenty percent of children and adolescents live in separated or divorced households,[8] and 20% of their parents' break-ups involve high-conflict situations that may be severe enough to lead to custody disputes. He then estimated that 25% of children and adolescents in high-conflict break-ups become alienated. Multiplying these values, he thus estimates that approximately 1% of children and adolescents have become alienated from at least one parent (740,000 cases in the U.S.), which is approximately the prevalence rate for autism spectrum disorder.[9]

Using a convenience sample of parents recruited on-line, our own research team asked 228 people whether they have known anyone who has exhibited particular parental alienating behaviors, and whether they themselves have been the target or perpetrator of such acts. Our results were shocking. Reports of witnessing others engaging in parental alienating behaviors ranged from 22.7% (forcing a child to reject the other parent or signal the child to not approach the other parent at an event) to 66.8% (yell at the other parent in front of a child). Among the 126 parents in the sample who were divorced or separated from the other parent, many reported being on the receiving end of numerous alienating behaviors: 14.3% of these parents reported that their child was forced to reject them by the other parent (low end), and 55.6% reported being yelled at by the other parent in front of a child. Between 21%-30% reported having their relationship minimized by the other parent, and many reported being the target of other negative behaviors (e.g., other parent told the child he or she was sick or dangerous, 29.4%). Even though these parenting behaviors are very negative, a number of respondents admitted to doing many of them themselves (e.g., 19.8% admitted to belittling the other parent in front of a child).[10]

We have recently partnered with Dr. Sadie Leder Elder of High Point University's Survey Research Center to complete the first known poll about parental alienation prevalence among a representative sample of North Carolina adults. Using a random sampling method, interviewers contacted 610 adults over the age of 18 years and asked them whether they are a parent or guardian to a child, and if they have been alienated from one or more of their children by the other parent. We found that 13% of the parents in the poll reported being the targets of parental alienation, which was 9% of the entire adult sample.[11] Extended to reflect prevalence in the U.S. general population, which is approximately 245,201,076 adults over the age of 18,[12] there are over 22 million adults in the U.S. alone who are currently being alienated from their children.

Explanatory research. Research can also be explanatory, in that the purpose is to understand or explain certain relationships. In other words, the researcher is interested in seeing what specific factors are related to each other, such as how personality traits, relationship milestones, and specific dynamics of relationships are related (or not) to parental alienating behaviors. For example, a researcher might conduct a survey of adult children from divorced families and ask about the alienating behaviors of their parent(s). They may also measure their current psychological well-being and examine whether past experience with alienation is related to their current psychological health. Likewise, the researcher might be interested in whether certain personality disorders predict the likelihood of alienating a child. This type of question starts to get at the "why" of the problem. We will review explanatory research on parental alienation throughout the course of this book so we will not present research findings in detail here.

Predictive research. Finally, predictive questions move beyond the "why" to understand the *precise* relationships between certain factors. For example, explanatory research may show that narcissism is related to parental alienating behaviors. To what extent? Predictive research would examine (with reliable measures) what *specific* levels of narcissism are associated with different levels of parental alienation or severity of child or family outcomes. In other words, the purpose of these types of research questions are to get at not just why things are happening, but *how exactly different factors influence each other.* So far, because there is not been a lot of research (yet) on parental alienation, we could not find many studies that asked predictive research questions.

The primary goal of all of these three research question types is to generate theories, which are explanations about what parental alienation is, what causes it, and what outcomes it produces. Scientists test research questions using a wide variety of methods. Three of the most commonly used are experimental, correlational, and qualitative methods. *Experiments* are the "gold standard" of research methods, particularly randomized and controlled experiments. The method also allows researchers to show cause and effect because they control for all factors in the study except for the factor they think is causing the outcome. For example, if we think that a particular drug causes aggression, we would conduct an experiment and randomly assign people to receive the drug or not. We would also hold everything else constant, like have participants take the drug in the same study environment (e.g., a laboratory). Although such experiments are the ideal and preferred form of research because it is the only method that can demonstrate cause and effect, they are not always feasible or ethical to conduct. For example, if we want to know whether court involvement causes increases in parental alienating behaviors, it would not be ethical to randomly send some parents to a courthouse to file various motions and have others not do so. It would also not be ethical to randomly assign children to join a family where alienation is happening versus where it is not, and then see what happens to their mental health.

Correlational and qualitative studies are more feasible to conduct when researching topics such as parental alienation because the purpose is to explore and demonstrate that there are relationships between certain variables and not others. *Correlational* studies typically entail surveying people about their personal traits, attitudes and/or experiences. This method can demonstrate not just whether relationships exist between factors, but also the strength of those relationships. If we are only wanting to explore whether certain relationships exist, such as whether age of the child at the time of divorce is related to how severe their alienation was, we can survey adult children of divorced families about these factors and see if they are significantly associated. We can also test whether certain factors *predict* specific outcomes, and even measure people over a series of time points to see whether specific factors consistently predict outcomes over time. When we show that patterns of predictors and outcomes occur consistently over time, we can have confidence that one *may* be causing the other.

Qualitative studies use a large number of methods, such as content analysis of written texts (e.g., case or legal records), analysis of focus group or interview transcripts, and interpretations of case history data. While these methods cannot show cause and effect, they *can* show (like correlational studies) whether relationships between certain factors exist. These types of studies are largely exploratory, as the researchers are often hoping to learn what the participants' experiences have been like in their samples. Based on the factors identified in these methods, the researcher then starts developing "why" questions that can be tested with empirical research methods (correlational or experimental).

The sampling problem

Finding people to study is an important limitation for almost all kinds of research. Ideally, you want the people you study to be representative of everyone like them. So if we are studying targets of parental alienation, we would hope to get a sample of people who are very similar to *all* targets of parental alienation. If we wanted to see how alienated children are affected, we would want the sample we select to resemble *all* alienated children. This task can be challenging to accomplish given that there have not yet been a large number of studies on this topic to clarify exactly who is vulnerable to this problem. We know parental alienation largely affects divorced and separated families, but we have also learned that it can happen in intact families too.[13] But at what proportions? What proportion of targeted and alienating parents are step-parents? There is much we need to know in order to know who to sample.

When a researcher has to recruit participants for parental alienation studies, another issue is where to find them. A significant proportion of descriptive research on parental alienation (so far) has been representative of extreme, or severe cases because they represent the experiences of parents who have been presenting themselves to clinicians or the judicial system for help. This sampling problem means that the results cannot be generalized well to other targeted parents experiencing milder forms of parental alienation or who have not sought help. This issue is not unique to parental alienation, as many studies on domestic violence have sampled women or men who have sought out services in cases of severe physical abuse; those not seeking services are not represented. While the moderate-to-severe cases will be of interest to legal and mental health professionals, we are also interested in the whole spectrum of alienating behaviors and how this not-so-innocent "game" may affect real children's lives, not to mention the lives of the parents who are being kept at an emotional and/or physical distance from their children.

Although our research team was one of the first to poll a representative sample of parents, our findings need to be replicated in other states and across entire nations to determine whether a 9% prevalence rate of adults (13% of parents) is accurate.[11] While we do have good, representative data on domestic violence, there has not yet been a larger scale survey using a nationally representative sample of adults to assess actual prevalence of parental alienating behaviors in the general public. Such a project is expensive, ranging from $7,000-$15,000 and is something we are in the process of pursuing. Obtaining accurate prevalence estimates for parental alienation is an important first step in addressing this problem.

Evaluating scientific merit

The question remains as to whether the methods used to study parental alienation are scientific or not. We feel it will be useful here to contrast research on parental alienation with research on domestic violence, which has not suffered the same "junk" science criticism. In order to be considered scientific, the method, whether descriptive, explanatory, or predictive, must have the following characteristics: it must be replicable, precise, falsifiable, and parsimoneous.[14]

Replicability means that another researcher can replicate the methods used by a researcher, repeat their study, and obtain similar results. Both domestic violence and parental alienation research typically employ surveys and interview methods, and there have been decades of research in *both* areas showing replicable patterns of predictors and consequences of the behaviors.

Precision entails having definitions of a concept that allow others to be able to use the same definition in their own research. While there is not general consensus on a single definition of parental alienation, there is generally agreement in what clusters of behaviors constitute it. Across nearly all the research we have reviewed so far, parental alienation has been clearly described in terms of how it differs from other behaviors such as estrangement, however reliable measures distinguishing these behaviors have not yet been developed. This problem does not mean that the parental alienation term is not precise; rather, researchers have not yet found accurate ways of measuring it.

While precision is an issue for nearly all scientific research that measures abstract concepts, the larger issue here is that many people deny that parental alienation exists at all, or have their own lay definitions of what *they* think parental alienation is. These gaps in understanding and perspective dramatically impact research results. For example, one research study found that clinicians who believed parental alienation was a problem were able to reliably identify cases when it was present in case scenarios that they reviewed. Unfortunately, *many mental health professionals also declined participation in the study because they did not believe in the parental alienation syndrome.*[15] Does this mean that the results of their study were not good? No. The researchers used a clear description of what parental alienation is, but they also uncovered reluctance of some clinicians to acknowledge its very existence (we will get to the why question later in this book).

Domestic violence is an umbrella term for many different abusive behaviors such as physical and emotional violence, financial abuse, coercion and control, date rape, and stalking.[16] The complexity of the definition poses challenges to researchers because factors (e.g., work-stress spillover) associated with one type of abuse (e.g., physical violence) may not generalize to other types (e.g., stalking). Lay definitions of abuse may also vary by participants. When we searched a scientific database for research studies on domestic violence, over 8,000 studies were identified (compared to only 270 for parental alienation). Due to the sheer amount of published studies on the topic, we could not conduct a thorough review of how domestic violence was defined in each study. However, we did notice a number of studies that either focused on specific types of violence, or defined the topic quite generally and provided examples to participants of what domestic violence is. We argue that there is similar variability in the quality of definitional precision across domestic violence and parental alienation research studies.

Falsifiability means that the theory used to test a research question is stated in such a way that it can be proven false. Due to the fact that there is currently less research on parental alienation than domestic violence research, there have not been as many theories about why or how it happens yet. A considerable amount of research on domestic violence has been descriptive as well, so it is arguable that *both* parental alienation and domestic violence research have suffered to some extent from the falsifiability problem. When the definitions of the behaviors being studied are not precise, they cannot be measured or tested accurately and this also leads to falsifiability issues. Given that parental alienation definitions are quite precise, this makes falsifiability greater than in studies where domestic violence is not defined clearly.

Parsimony means that if there are multiple explanations for a behavior, the researcher selects the simplest or most logical explanation. From our reviews of the research on both topics, parental alienation and domestic violence research are not very dissimilar in their parsimoniousness. Both bodies of research have identified and tested specific factors associated with their outcomes, and many of the proposed and tested relationships were drawn from initial qualitative research (e.g., interviews). Although there are a number of factors that have been associated with parental alienating behaviors, we have not seen studies proposing multiple and complex webs of factors that explain the behavior-- most have been quite simple and clear.

In summary, *scientific evidence for parental alienation is not based on junk science*. Research in this area is new, and therefore what has been published so far has been largely descriptive and predictive in nature. The irony we see in the argument that research on parental alienation as being "junk" lies in the fact that the methods used to study it so far have not been much different than those used to study domestic violence, a scientifically accepted phenomenon. Like parental alienation, it would not be ethical to randomly assign people to particular relationships where there is an abuser to see what happens to victims. We must rely on cases where domestic violence or parental alienation exists in its varying forms and see what the predictors and consequences are. Given such staunch denial by many about whether parental alienation is even real, it is no wonder that the majority of the research so far has focused on documenting its existence, its impact on mental and physical health outcomes, and perceptions of judicial and clinical professionals working with clients coping with the problem.

In chapter 1, we discussed having conducted a large, qualitative interview study of our own to explore parental alienation as a way to better understand not only *what* is going on (descriptive), but *why* (predictive). That said, this book does not serve as a formal report on our research findings. In the near future, we will be employing stringent qualitative analysis techniques on those interview transcripts in order to examine specific research questions for scientific publication. Rather, the purpose of this book is to provide a review and reframing of this issue. To do this, we will be presenting research findings on parental alienation and other social science research, and offer evidence from our own interviews to support and bolster the associations that others have found.

We recognize there are limitations to all research methods, but it is important to note that when multiple studies with different samples and different research methods report similar patterns of results (e.g., the association between narcissism and parental alienating behaviors), then we have confidence that there *is* an important relationship there. Indeed, a critical review of research on parental alienation research has discussed that even though studies to date have varied in methodological rigor, there is concordance and consensus across studies that makes their findings reliable. Research so far demonstrates with confidence that it *does* exist, and that there are a number of findings that are based on empirically sound methods.[17] Again, this research area is in its infancy, and there is much more work that needs to be done. In this book we will review research studies that have a sound methodological basis and/or have been replicated in some form. We argue that parental alienation is the new domestic violence of our time, and it needs to be uncovered, recognized, researched, and treated with the same respect.

CHAPTER FOUR

WHO ARE THESE ALIENATORS?

Benjamin Garber eloquently stated that parental alienation occurs due to a "perfect storm of relationship dynamics."[1] These dynamics include a child's exposure to a parent who says horrible and demeaning things about the other parent (e.g., "your dad is not here to pick you up on time, he does not care about you"), the child's direct experience with the other parent (e.g., "dad is late all the time"), and an unhealthy relationship with the alienating parent (e.g., "mom loves me more than dad"). Who *are* these people who alienate their children from a loving parent?

Our research indicates that alienators may be individuals who have been unable to accept the end of the relationship or marriage to the other parent (even if they ended it themselves), and they unconsciously or consciously want to maintain some sort of continuing bond with them. These parents also blame the other parent for their own state of misery.[2] Many alienators come to believe that the other parent offers no value to their children, that they are "dangerous" and "abusive," and that they do not care for or love their children.[3]

These parents seem to lack insight into how their behaviors are contributing to the problem, and oftentimes point fingers and blame the other parent for what they themselves are doing. While these behaviors are done on an individual basis, they are often supported and encouraged by friends, family, courts, and other institutions.

A number of other individual characteristics have been associated with parental alienating behaviors. Gender has been a controversial issue because some research has found no gender difference in who alienates[4] while others have found substantial differences. For example, researchers have found that mothers have more influence than fathers to change a child's affection towards another parent or step-parent, and are more effective at sabotaging their relationship(s).[5] Much of the discrepancy in research findings about gender as an important factor lies in how the studies themselves were conducted (e.g., how participants were selected) and in how custody is awarded or changed over time.

Custodial status

The custodial parent is more likely and easily able to influence children, so parental alienation is most commonly done by them.[6] This fact is one of the reasons for recent legislative pushes to promote equal parenting time after divorce unless there is **legitimate** evidence of one parent being unfit. Mothers are granted sole or primary custody of children after divorce over 70-80% of the time across the world,[7] so this has been used to explain why mothers are most often the alienators. Indeed, an extensive review of family case law in Canada found that mothers were the alienating parent in 68% of the cases.[8] Therefore, the way custody is allocated largely explains why there are gender differences in who the alienators are, so our legal institutions play a strong hand in the perpetuation of this issue.

In a research study examining how satisfied parents are with custodial decisions made by the courts, fathers were found to be generally satisfied with their custody arrangement when mothers have primary custody of children, *as long as there is not high conflict.* That is, conflict, discord, or hostility are often present when fathers are dissatisfied.[9] We do not believe that awarding shared custody (e.g., 50/50) will create additional conflict; many other factors play a role in whether there is conflict between parents than actual custodial arrangements.

An important and sometimes controversial topic related to custody is the granting of overnight stays to both parents of a baby. Many child developmentalists (including Dr. Biringen) have written highly cited articles about the importance of maintaining stability of sleeping arrangements for a baby, and to only gradually increase nighttime parenting at different homes in the very early years of life. Dr. Biringen continues to believe that this is important for an infant to develop a sense of stability, unlike the recommendations of some psychologists that infants need to "switch" residences after 3-4 days lest they forget the love and caring of the other parent. However, this belief is predicated on the fact that both parents would "do right" by their children and promote a positive relationship with the non-custodial parent during these early years. *If a conflictual situation is brewing and can insidiously take hold, or parental alienation is clearly occurring, a monopoly on overnights and custody is not a healthy recommendation for the child.*

Desire for a "clean slate"

Parental alienation sometimes begins with a parent who wants to start life over without forever being connected to the other parent. Wanting a "clean break," such a parent is more likely to initiate the alienation process. She or he may be coached by friends, family, or their lawyers to make claims about child abuse ("She neglects the children and does not feed them"), domestic violence ("We are afraid to be near him") or mental illness ("She is crazy"). The underlying reasons for this are covered later in this book, but one needs to understand that many alienators do this deliberately and for strategic purposes, such as to get more child custody and support, or to harass and "punish" the targeted parent. Some of the parents we interviewed described their alienators as *appearing* like well-functioning, "upstanding citizens" (e.g., attorneys, physicians, teachers), yet they were highly erratic and hostile behind the scenes. Some parents started their alienation because they had a new romantic partner and perceived continuing to "share" a family with the targeted parent as an inconvenience. Others simply wanted revenge after their relationship failed.

New relationship status

Many of the targeted mothers we interviewed were step-mothers. Being a step-parent is not typically an easy role for any person to take on, and alienating parents often made this particularly difficult for the new step-parent. Many fathers described alienating behaviors increasing in severity after they remarried, and that their new wives were regularly attacked by their ex-wives, either professionally (e.g., mocking her during public speaking events; attacking her reputation on-line) or personally (e.g., turning friends and teachers against her). We also interviewed mothers who were targeted by step-mothers-- in fact most mothers believed that parental alienation would not be happening had their ex-husband not remarried. New girlfriends or step-mothers often were in cahoots with an alienating father in telling untruths about the mother (e.g., "Boy, she *is* really crazy"). New boyfriends or step-fathers sometimes assisted alienating mothers in these tactics as well, such as by physically blocking access to the children during parenting exchanges when it was the targeted parent's parenting time. Targeted parents also told us of a few cases in which the alienating parent behaved "nicely" whenever they started dating someone new—they wanted to look like a good and cooperative co-parent to their new romantic partner. However, once their relationship ended, the parent swiftly returned to their alienating tactics. Therefore, changes in relationship status over time can strongly influence the severity of the alienating tactics used by the parent.

Inability to cope with loss

When the parents' relationship ends, dislike and even hatred oftentimes remain. The parents are left with one of two options. The sophisticated, "high road" option is to sit with conflicting emotions: the parent does not love or even like the other parent anymore, but they want their children to have a loving relationship and connection with them. This option requires some ability or capacity of the parent to be reflective and empathetic. The other, more primitive option, is an either/or scenario. The parent says "I don't like them, and so my children cannot like them either." Simply put, it is too threatening or difficult for the parent to have different members of the same family unit feeling different emotions, so she or he influences the child to adopt the same viewpoint.[10] Avoiding conflicting emotions and not appreciating that life contains a lot of gray rather than simple black/white dichotomies, is a more primitive way of coping than to consciously face and resolve disparate ways of thinking or feeling.

Social network members such as family members, friends, mental health professionals, and medical providers may inadvertently reinforce the alienator's dichotomous ways of thinking about the world. When an alienating parent complains about how horrible the targeted parent is, how quickly are these individuals to believe their opinion (with little to no evidence), especially when he or she idealized and loved the targeted parent just months or years before? We heard many targeted parents describe how others would support the alienator's perspective without hearing their other side of the story or thinking critically about what was being said about them. For example, one targeted mother described how all of her co-workers stopped inviting her out to happy hours after work because they believed many lies her ex-husband told them about her. She was shocked that people she had known for many years believed him, and the consequence was that she felt very isolated from those she had considered friends. Therefore, social networks can be active or passive participants in the promotion of alienation by supporting (or not even challenging) the dichotomous thinking of the parent who is advertently or inadvertently alienating their children. One of the purposes of this book is to create awareness within society that this problem exists and that *what one hears from one source (e.g., a spiteful parent) is not the only version of the truth.*

When the relationship ends, this event can also trigger unresolved feelings of grief and loss in the alienating parent. This loss can trigger an unconscious belief that their emotional needs can be met by over-connecting with their children, something called *compulsive caregiving.*[11] This form of caregiving "proves" the parent's worthiness because they are then not as unlovable as they feel. The compulsive caregiver becomes overly concerned with the safety of the children, particularly in the presence of the other parent or their extended family. For example, a mother may tell others that she is scared to leave her children with their father for extended periods of time because she doesn't know whether he will give them their prescribed medicines. Regardless of the specifics of how this would be portrayed in any family, many alienating parents are over-connected with their children.

Compulsive self-reliance is another unhealthy response to loss, and this is related to the idea that a motive of alienating parents is to seek a clean slate. In their grief, these individuals cut off all ties or resemblance of ties to the person they were once emotionally connected to. These parents set an example for the child that they should sever all ties with the other parent as well. Parents with compulsive self-reliance would not likely agree or cooperate with co-parenting or shared parenting arrangements because they believe that they are the *only* parent who can effectively raise the children. They do not trust the other parent or want to have any form of relationship with them anymore.

Personality disorders

Many parents who alienate their children have personality disorders, which are pervasive patterns of "inner experience and behavior" that are different than what is considered "normal."[12] These patterns are typically evident and stable since adolescence, and result in what are called "adaptive failures" in thought, emotions, interpersonal functioning, and impulse control. Biases in thoughts and feelings can trigger underlying feelings of insecurity and threat, and this is exacerbated by the separation or loss of their relationship with the other parent.

Legal and clinical professionals have suggested that if there is a parent with a personality disorder who also has a strong hatred and obsession towards the other parent, then accusations about abuse should be distrusted unless there is strong, corroborating evidence. Indeed, in a review of 181 case files from contested divorce and custody cases where there were false accusations of sexual abuse, the falsely accusing parent was significantly more likely to have a personality disorder than in cases where there were no false allegations.[13]

Parents with personality disorders may appear "healthy" at work or in their public life, but they show the defining features of their disorder in their private lives. They may appear to outsiders as having it "all together," but they are unwilling and unable to take the perspective of others, including that of their child. Therefore, they cannot provide consistent support to their children in a way that is truly in their best interests.

When children feel they can trust their parent to be there for them when they are feeling distressed, and learn through their relationship that they have value and self-worth, they develop what we call a *secure attachment* to them. Parents with personality disorders, or who have many symptoms of them, are unable to do this. As a result, their children develop an *insecure attachment*, which is a distorted view of the world and of the people in it. These children start using the same primitive coping strategies that their alienating parent uses for coping with stress, such as viewing people as either good or bad (and nothing in between) and denying their own role in problems. When there is no or limited contact with the targeted parent, who might be healthier and could counteract or neutralize such pathological coping strategies, these children are isolated in an alternative reality. We interviewed many parents who had to confront their children's rage about events from their life that never occurred, but were adamantly believed due to what the alienating parent had told them.

While there are several disorders that are associated with parental alienation tactics, the most common are borderline, narcissistic, and antisocial personality disorders.

Borderline personality disorders (BPD)

This personality disorder is characterized by severe emotional instability that leads to many other social and behavioral problems. Individuals with BPD often have a negative self-image and very low self-esteem and self-worth. Although these individuals want loving, close relationships, their feelings of worthlessness result in frequent mood swings, anger and hostility, and impulsiveness that ultimately pushes others away. Individuals with BPD often idealize people one day, and then hate them with a vengeance the next. They also can experience stress-related paranoia and dissociative thoughts, meaning that they lose a sense of reality. Even minor events like changes in plans or going on a family vacation can trigger severe mood fluctuations.

According to the National Institute of Mental Health, there are genetic and developmental factors (e.g., unstable and traumatic early relationships) that are associated with BPD, and it affects about 1.6% of adults in the U.S.[14] Many professionals believe that this prevalence rate is underestimated because people with BPD also often have other mental illnesses such as depression. Most clinicians will not report both diagnoses, and will instead only report or treat the disorder that can be treated with medication (such as depression). There is no medical treatment for BPD, but intensive psychotherapy has been effective, that is, if the individual believes they need it. Unfortunately, individuals with BPD rarely feel they need treatment, or they change therapists as soon as they are challenged by them to address their underlying issues.

The erratic, hostile, and impulsive behaviors BPD individuals express with adults are also expressed with their children. These parents oftentimes appear as very involved and place their children on a pedestal--at least, until they feel let down by them. Children of BPD parents are highly vulnerable to emotional, verbal, and physical abuse because their parent shares intense and inappropriate anger when they believe they have been treated "unfairly," were disrespected, or let-down by them. These parents, particularly BPD mothers, need excessive reassurance from their children that they will not abandon them, and this is most evident when the children are in their adolescent years.[15] Unfortunately, adolescence is an important time for children to become more independent from their parents, so the consequences on an adolescent child's identity development are *very* negative.

One example of BPD parenting was described by an alienated father we interviewed. His teenage daughter, who was very over-connected with her BPD mother, posted a video onto social media that was viewed as inappropriate by the BPD mother. His healthy response was to communicate with his daughter about the dangers of social media and create a social media contract to set boundaries and expectations about what is considered appropriate. The BPD mother, however, overreacted by verbally attacking the child by phone and with incessant text messages, pulled her out of class at school to shame her in front of her friends, told her that she had thrown out all of her shorts and skirts that were cut above the knee, and banned her from social media for a year. The daughter was devastated, until 3 days later the mother retracted the punishment and they were once again 'best friends.' We heard many stories like this about BPD mothers in our interviews.

BPD parents also have unrealistic expectations for how much time they should spend with their child and are driven to have their own needs met through their relationship with them. These parents usually project onto their children their own unresolved family problems, making it very hard for them to be emotionally available to them.[16] For example, a mother of three daughters may alienate the dad because it recreates a hostile dynamic the mother had with her sisters and father when she herself was a child in her family of origin. Sadly, this dynamic creates an unhealthy relationship with the children, or what clinicians we discussed earlier called an "unholy alliance." When a child has a normal emotional reaction to something, such as crying when they are scared, BPD parents get stuck in defensive thought patterns and become extremely overprotective and intrusive with them. This cognitive trap that the BPD parent falls into makes it hard for the child to integrate their feelings with their behaviors, which can lead to arrested or stunted emotional development.[17]

When children are raised by a parent with BPD, they may develop what clinicians call *disorganized attachment*,[18] and this can make coping with stress and emotional regulation difficult for them. The BPD parent's low feelings of self-worth are transferred to the child, who is then raised with a very distorted, unpredictable, and fragile identity, similar to their parent with borderline personality disorder. These children may also start externalizing their behaviors, which can come across to teachers and others as attention-deficit (ADHD) or conduct disorders. They are also at high risk for developing severe forms of psychological illnesses and grandiose forms of narcissism due to the excessive intrusiveness and unusual closeness with the BPD parent.

When BPD parents are interviewed by clinicians, they generally rate their family and relationships more negatively than healthy family members do because they feel defensive about being assessed.[19] *Inexperienced clinicians may also interpret the over-connectedness and idealization of their children as normal parenting behaviors rather than as symptoms of their disorder.* Multiple viewpoints should be used when conducting a clinical assessment of families for this reason. Most custody evaluations, however, do not include extensive and thorough psychiatric evaluations of both parents, or conduct thorough interviews of people from both sides of the family. Although this personality disorder is an important predictor of risk for parental alienation, it is rarely assessed.

Narcissistic personality disorder (NPD)

This personality disorder is characterized by a person who has an excessive and exaggerated feeling of self-importance and preoccupation with themselves. They also have a nearly complete lack of empathy for others and a strong sense of entitlement. People with NPD may look confident, but also arrogant, and they oftentimes brag about their abilities and accomplishments with the belief that only other great people will really understand and value them. All others suffer from mediocrity.[20]

Narcissists demand empathy from others, yet cannot grant the same in return. They demand constant and unwavering attention, are preoccupied with fantasies about "ideal" love and success, and pursue selfish goals. They are very sensitive to criticism due to intense feelings of shame, so when they perceive that someone does not value them, this creates a lot of interpersonal conflict. Similar to people with BPD, they idealize people one day (when they believe they are being treated the way they should be) and lash back with anger, shame, and humiliation the next when they feel undervalued.[21] One targeted mother we interviewed reported on how her NPD ex-husband demanded complete obedience of the children, and if any deviated from his expectations for how children "should" behave, they were severely punished. Oftentimes, people in relationships with narcissists are left feeling used.

In a study comparing attempts to negotiate parenting plans between divorced parents, Marion Ehrenberg and her colleagues found that NPD parents were likely to disagree with *any* proposed plan, were not able to take the other parent's perspective, were not very concerned about the welfare of everyone involved (particularly the children), and they prioritized their own needs above others.[22] These parents oftentimes shower their children with attention because they idealize them and "know what is best," yet they fail to recognize the negative impact of this behavior on the child. They also feel great neediness and excessive longing when they are not with their child, which showcases how they are taking more than they are giving in their relationship.

Because NPD parents express their love for their children quite inconsistently, their children are at high risk for developing psychological disorders themselves.[23] NPD parents use children as possessions that can be controlled, bullied, and manipulated to get what they want. NPD parents live through their children, yet this is for their own self-validation, not for their child's benefit. They may be happy when their child succeeds, but on some unconscious level they may also be worried about being overshadowed by them. These parents may create and change rules at their own discretion, sometimes just to feel the power they have in the situation. They may believe they can do no wrong and that the targeted parent is always wrong, is "crazy," or a "deadbeat." They may lie to achieve their goals and create a picture of being "perfect." They may use blackmail and dominate conversations with stories about themselves. Overinvolved, controlling parents create narcissistic children, so the disorder is transmitted from one generation to the next.[24]

NPD is more common among men than women,[25] and men who have it tend to be more exploitative and feel more 'entitled' than women. Behaviors and outcomes for NPD men and women, however, are generally the same.[26] In her book about parental alienation, Amy Baker lists narcissistic mothers in both intact and divorced families as being likely to alienate the other parent, but 1 in 6 fathers also were characterized as narcissistic and likely to exhibit the same behaviors.[27]

Antisocial/psychopathic personality disorder

Many people who have personality disorders have more than one. Aside from BPD and NPD, a large number of alienating parents also show signs of having antisocial/psychopathic personality disorders. People with this disorder have inflated grandiosity (much like narcissists) and a general pattern of lying, violating the rights of others, as well as breaking the law. They are characterized as being callous, deceitful, manipulative, and hostile. While narcissists lie to get what they want, this group is even more skilled in this quality and they lack empathy for the damage they do. Those with antisocial/psychopathic personalities are over-represented among criminal offenders and they tend to engage in predatory behaviors such as stalking or harassing. Many parents we interviewed reported that the alienating parent constantly followed them on social media, had others spy on them, vandalized their property, and were obsessed with their comings and goings.

One father we interviewed reported that his ex-wife repeatedly attempted to get him fired from his job and convinced his children to make false claims of child abuse to people who were mandatory reporters (e.g., school counselors) so that she could get custody. Another mother reported to us how her ex-husband successfully manipulated her children to claim they did not want to ever see her again and he doctored email exchanges to make it appear that she was harassing and threatening him. He also convinced the judicial system (with no evidence) that the mother was abusive, neglectful, and a threat to her own children, despite the fact that he himself had been jailed for domestic violence before their divorce. Her custodial rights were subsequently revoked because the courts believed the false evidence and claims he provided to them.

Alienating parents may never have been arrested or have a criminal record, but those with this personality disorder will show these pathological signs in their interpersonal relationships. A large number of alienating parents are able to manipulate and "work the system" to block the healthier parent's access to the children. Most alienating parents are actually breaking the law by violating court ordered parenting plans, and they get away with this by manipulating a large number of people who have the ability to influence how courts enforce them (e.g., teachers, police officers). Such professionals are not often knowledgeable about this personality disorder and so the parental alienator's behaviors go unrecognized as being problematic. As a result, the alienator continues to get away with their behaviors. The level of disregard for honest and ethical behavior, as well as extensive social manipulation of others (including the children) are unique trademarks of this personality disorder. This may be a new face of alienation.

Features of these personality disorders

All three of these personality disorders are diagnosed when individuals present a significant level of pathology. Research has indicated, however, that even when a parent has only a few symptoms of these disorders (and not a full-blown diagnosis), their relationships with their children may still be affected. For example, mothers with only a few features of BPD are more emotionally unavailable to their children than those diagnosed with the clinical disorder.[28] If a child is being raised by a parent who tends to see the world in only black and white terms (good/bad), their child will also be raised to think, feel, and interpret the world in the same extreme ways. Optimal child rearing involves having the ability to engage in a lot of self-reflection, and having the capacity to monitor one's own thinking and emotions (which psychologists refer to as *meta-cognitive ability*).[29] In lay terms, it means the parent should have the capacity to objectively evaluate their own actions and feelings, as if they were an outside observer. Many parents with personality disorders are not capable of such objectivity, but it would be in their children's best interests if they could.

Enmeshment

Another important characteristic of the alienating parent, whether they have a personality disorder or not, is that they oftentimes have a strong and dependent relationship with the alienated child, something clinicians call *enmeshment*. Many of our interviewees described the alienating parent as lacking boundaries[30] and of isolating their children from others, including extended family. The result is the development and maintenance of a 'microworld' where the child perceives the alienating parent as the only safe and trusting person they know.

Further, the child is placed in an inappropriate role: as a peer, "best friend," confidante, or even an inappropriate spousal role. Although there is great cultural variability in how much dependency is normal between parents and children, with greater dependency common in individuals from cultures such as Israelis[31] and Hispanic Americans,[32] the behaviors described in cases of parental alienation are extreme in comparison to norms in such cultures.

One of the fathers we interviewed noted enmeshment between his son and the mother from very early on. Rather than attending their public school, the mother wanted her son to be homeschooled and associate solely with other homeschooled children and families. Over time, the mother built a homeschooling microcosm in their town, in which the members all supported one another's viewpoints about education away from the mainstream. This group also promoted a misunderstanding of *attachment parenting*, such that members slept in the same bed with their children from infancy to late adolescence rather than having the practice end much earlier in the child's development. After his divorce, the father reported the mother to social services because she was still sleeping in the same bed as her adolescent son. Social services did not intervene. Had the situation been reversed, with a father sleeping in the same bed as an adolescent daughter, he likely would have lost custody of her due to gender biases held by the social workers.

Normal boundary setting of the healthy (oftentimes targeted parent) parent, such as limiting the amount of texting or phone calls between children and the alienating parent during their parenting time is often perceived by enmeshed parents as "interference." Many of the targeted parents we spoke to reported not being able to communicate with their children at all when they were with the alienating parent, and yet when the children were with them, the alienator was in *constant* communication with the children, not being able to let a day or two (or even hours) go by without having some contact with them (e.g., sending pictures, asking questions that could wait until they see them again). These enmeshed parents will often accuse the targeted parent of alienating them from their children when they set such boundaries, however their interference is the actual alienation.

Money, control, and domination

In our interviews with mothers and fathers, we asked each parent what they feel motivates their ex's parental alienating behaviors. The most common responses to this question were *money* and *control*. Money was described as relating to the desire of the alienator to have all custody for child support purposes. Some parents were so enmeshed with their children that they used this as evidence of not being able to work-- their children "needed" them too much. After making such claims, these alienating parents often demanded in court that they needed lifetime maintenance or alimony from the other parent.

By having control of the children, the alienator has control over the targeted parent. The targeted parent simply wants a healthy, loving relationship with their children; the alienator controls (or attempts to control) how often, when, and where the targeted parent can even communicate with them. The alienator is in a powerful position, and they do not give it up easily, particularly parents with personality disorders. These parents measure their success by their ability to completely sever their children's relationship with the other parent.[33] For example, many targeted parents reported that they could rarely speak or communicate electronically with their children when they were with the alienator, as the alienator either restricted, intercepted or blocked their communication attempts. Alienators sometimes provide very tight windows when the targeted parent can call, and yet find it unacceptable when the other parent suggests imposing similar restrictions when the children are with them.

When there are severe restrictions in contact imposed by the alienating parent (and not by the court), many targeted parents have no recourse but to involve the courts to enforce child custody and visitation orders. This intervention creates substantial financial burdens and stress on the targeted parent. The conscious or unconscious intention of causing harm and injury to the targeted parent then becomes a "testing of wills" to see if the other can survive financially. When the targeted parent does not have money or resources to seek court assistance, alienating parents often accuse them of not caring about the kids, or tell the children that their mom or dad "signed over all rights" and abandoned them. One mother we interviewed was forced to have supervised visits (with a mental health professional) with her children due to false accusations made about abusing her children. She was working three jobs to pay off over $70,000 in legal expenses accumulated while trying to get unsupervised visits restored. Several wealthy parents that we interviewed could barely make ends meet because they had to allocate almost all of their money for legal expenses just to be able to see their children. Although courts will enforce child support and spousal maintenance payments (e.g., garnishment of wages, detention in jail), they rarely enforce ordered parenting time. Due to this disparity, the custodial parent has much more control in this situation than the parent with less parenting time.

Many targeted parents described to us how their children "jumped" when the other parent wanted or required something. For example, one father described how his kids began to get very tense near custody exchange times-- they did not want to be even slightly late because it would make their mother upset. The alienating parent is often described as dominant in presence, a "terrorist," and needing only to look askance for the children to want to comply with any said or unsaid demands.

We know little about the alienator's perspective, as it is difficult to get anyone to admit to being an alienator. These parents believe on some level that they are doing what is in their children's best interests. Given that many alienators likely have undiagnosed or untreated personality disorders or features of personality disorders that do not fully meet DSM-5 criteria, they often derive some unconscious satisfaction in hurting and ostracizing the targeted parent. They are also likely empowered by the allegiance their children demonstrate towards them and feel vindicated as being the "better" parent and worthy of love because of it.

We interviewed only one parent who admitted to having been an alienator for the majority of her child's life, and she now lived with considerable guilt about it. She saw the impact that her behaviors had on her child, and how her daughter's adult relationships now reflect the conflict that she perpetuated for many years. To cope with her past, this mother attended many support groups for single mothers and told her story. She provided advice to mothers who she believed were alienating their children from the fathers, and she said that many mothers had no idea that what they were doing was wrong. We are hoping that all mothers and fathers read this book and become aware that it is a gift (rather than a burden) to raise a child who is loved by both parents. Children suffer intensely when they are led to believe they have been abandoned by the other parent or that there is something terribly wrong with them. These beliefs are devastating and traumatic for children to cope with for their entire lives.

We also hope that with greater awareness, mothers and fathers will start seeing that such behaviors are a form of aggression, just like domestic violence, and that they need to *stop for the sake of their children*! We know that many will not stop because subconscious motivations, such as those present among people with personality disorders and pathological responses to coping with grief, lead to illogical reasoning and decision-making among alienators. Many of these parents use primitive defense mechanisms and adamantly believe the other parent is bad, an abuser, unhealthy, a horrible influence, and better off not being in their children's lives. Psychologists often argue that these types of parents are very difficult to work with and successful clinical interventions with them are rare.[34]

How are these alienating behaviors enacted over time? Are there any major turning points, or milestones that influence whether the alienation increases? We turn to these questions next.

CHAPTER FIVE

HOW ARE ALIENATING BEHAVIORS ENACTED

OVER TIME?

Over the course of our interviews, we heard many examples of alienating behaviors designed to distance parents from their children. We have purposefully omitted here a full listing of alienating behaviors because they have been well documented by past researchers. Suffice it to say, these behaviors range considerably in terms of types of behaviors (e.g., restriction in communication to emotional manipulation) and severity (e.g., limiting phone calls to moving away with the children and not providing a forwarding address). Instead we will discuss here on how alienating behaviors change over time, and some of the strategies alienating parents use to accomplish their aims.

Early and insidious signs

When asked to recall when the first signs of alienation were occurring, we heard many parents say that they had no idea it was happening until things got really bad, such as now having no contact with their children at all. Most parents did not know that there was a term for what they were experiencing until they started doing research on the internet. Upon reflection of events that led up to their current situation, parents identified a number of early signs that the seeds of parental alienation were being planted--oftentimes well before the dissolution of the relationship with the alienator. This fact is important, as parental alienating behaviors may occur before there is a high conflict divorce. We have heard many parents and professionals equate parental alienation with high conflict divorces or relationships, however they are unique (albeit often related) terms.

If the targeted parent had limited time with the children while in the relationship, the alienator usually had the opportunity to develop a stronger (though not necessarily more healthy) bond with them. This early bond allows the alienator to have a larger and more powerful/influential presence in the children's lives. For example, several targeted parents that we interviewed described how the alienator would take the children out for dinners, vacations, or other events, and deliberately exclude them. This gradual distancing resulted in the targeted parent feeling greater disconnection from their children over time, even before the relationship ended.

Another early sign of parental alienation was the use of isolation tactics. Many alienators have anxiety or depression, which can result in a preference to stay home rather than develop or maintain social relationships outside of their family. These parents then use guilt to pressure the other parent in to isolating themselves as well. One targeted parent described having organized many parties and social events in and outside of the home during his marriage, and his then-wife would fake migraines and other illnesses in order to avoid interacting with their friends. She also frequently cancelled plans at the last minute with friends they shared in common, which eventually lead to the destruction of those relationships.

Many early stage alienators also demanded that the other parent distance themselves or break off their relationships with extended family because they were perceived by them as being unsupportive, unhealthy, or as not liking him (or her). For example, one mother we interviewed was given an ultimatum by her then-husband after her daughter was born--either disown her mother or he would leave her. To keep the peace in her new family, she promptly distanced herself from her mother. Unfortunately, when her marriage ended, she then did not have the support of her own family to cope with the alienation. Using similar isolation strategies, this alienating father turned his attention to distancing the children from her and it was then that she recognized that the alienation had been going on well before their marital separation.

Some targeted parents were not happy with the behaviors of the alienator even when they were together, but they played along or passively accepted it in order to preserve their marriage and be there for their children. One father we spoke with knew the mother had borderline personality disorder, was severely alienating the children from him, and was extremely hostile and aggressive towards him. This father remained in the house and refused to leave or file for divorce because he knew that if he did, she would never let him see his children again.

Using social networks to alienate

Illustrated in a few of the examples we have provided so far, many alienators enlist family to assist in their campaign against the other parent. This tactic is particularly evident in cultures where maintaining family and community relationships are of utmost priority. For example, among Arabs in the Middle East, divorce is viewed as an insult to the mother's extended family, who are primarily responsible for helping the mother after a divorce. Therefore, Arab Israeli targeted parents (usually fathers) field considerable hostility and slanderous remarks made about them by not only the alienating parent, but their extended family.[1] In such contexts, parental alienation is an entire family affair.

We found the involvement of extended family to be common in many of our interviews as well, particularly when the alienator does not remarry. Ex-mother-in-law's, in particular, were often co-conspirators in the alienator's campaign against the targeted parent. One father we interviewed reported that he had a very hard time connecting with his children and that his daughter rarely called him "Daddy." Although he could not describe exactly what his ex-wife was saying or doing to accomplish her alienation, his ex-mother-in-law would openly and blatantly badmouth and criticize him in front of the children when he would pick them up for his visits. In this case, the grandmother played the role of the alienating parent and the mother did not discourage her behavior.

Alienators also enlist other important adults in children's lives, such as neighbors, friends, teachers, and athletic coaches. Many parents we interviewed described how the attitudes of teachers towards them would change dramatically after the alienating parent "poisoned" their perception of them. For example, one father was welcomed into the classroom to volunteer for several weeks at the beginning of the school year until his ex-wife learned of it. Then, suddenly, the teacher told him that he was not welcome in the class anymore and that communication between them should be fully mediated by his ex-wife. He was not sure what the teacher had been told about him, and he was not able to correct any misperceptions she was led to believe. This type of situation was described by a large number of the alienated parents we interviewed.

Even adults who are trying to help address conflict between parents can make matters worse. For example, leading and suggestive questioning of children made by evaluators and court-appointed mediators can result in invalid reports of abuse.[2] There is considerable research on human memory indicating that false memories are easily created by mental and medical health professionals.[3] Indeed, Stephen Ceci and Maggie Bruck found in a series of experiments that even when young girls were fully clothed during a physical exam with a doctor, suggestive questioning about the exam resulted in them later believing that the doctor had touched their genitals and even stuck things inside of their vaginas.[2] Therefore, while adults may believe they are being helpful in assessing abuse, the way in which they ask questions and make suggestions can actually change the child's memory and recollection of events.

Escalating events

Many people believe that parental alienating behaviors escalate at the time the relationship ends (e.g., the divorce) and then subside. This belief is not true in a large number of cases. Often, alienation begins during the marriage, and intact families are not immune to this relationship tactic.[4] Alienating behaviors also have the potential to become chronic and can continue well into the adult years of the children in the family.

We found evidence in our interviews that alienating behaviors often escalate around particular life events, namely when there were important court dates related to custody or financial disputes, or when the targeted parent begins a new relationship. In some cases, alienating behaviors increased when the alienator himself/herself started a new romantic relationship. We learned from one parent that flurries of anonymous calls to Child Protective Services (CPS) with false claims of abuse would "coincidentally" occur around major events related to court disputes and when his relationship with his new wife became more serious (e.g., when they moved in together, after they were engaged). Once supervisors finally took notice of this pattern and addressed the alienating parent about her behavior, the calls miraculously stopped. This parent then started directing her alienation tactics in other ways, such as by brainwashing the children into believing (tragic) family events—events that never actually happened.

Awareness of the impact of parental alienation

We interviewed many parents who, despite severe alienation, did not reciprocate the alienating parent's behaviors because they had an awareness that *doing so was very harmful to their children.* One father very consciously described the positive characteristics of his ex-wife to his children: she was a great cook, she was smart, and their mutual love of rock climbing brought them together. He also told his kids that their mother was doing the best she could. He explicitly wanted his kids to have fond memories of their mother and relied on indirect strategies to illustrate that she often spoke untruths. When his son said, "You're a liar, you did not live on the beach in Florida" the father responded with, "Yes, we had a beach house; just check with mom that we lived on the beach in Florida and that she enjoyed living by the water." Telling his son that his ex-wife was lying was perceived by this father as the same as calling her a liar, and he did not want to alienate him from her the way she was doing it to him. Rather, he pointed out facts and truths (however basic) that could be verified for accuracy by the mother and at other times he told his son that he just had a different version of the story than what his mother told him.

Have you, or someone you know, ever engaged in alienating behaviors? Many people alienate to get back at their spouse or ex-partner, but they may not be aware they are ultimately harming their children. It is sometimes tempting to say negative things about an ex-partner, but little ears are often listening and the badmouthing is interpreted by them as being about them, not the other parent. Parents, whether in intact relationships with the other parent or not, need to be very mindful of how they speak to and about each other in front of children (or within earshot). *These conversations send clear messages to children about their own value as human beings.*

Parental alienating behaviors and strategies change considerably over time, and children are more vulnerable at different points in their lives. We will next explore how the relationship with the alienator and the alienating behaviors themselves affect children.

CHAPTER SIX

WHAT KIND OF RELATIONSHIP DO ALIENATED

CHILDREN HAVE WITH THE ALIENATOR AND

HOW DOES THIS AFFECT THEM?

Parental alienation is tragic. A considerable amount of research and public discourse on parental alienation likens it to a form of child emotional abuse. If child emotional abuse involves deliberate tactics to psychologically frighten a child ("your mother is abusive, neglectful, unsafe"), to humiliate a child ("he does not love you"), or to isolate a child ("you cannot go there to be with her"), then we agree. Here, we describe factors that increase a child's vulnerability to alienation. These factors highlight fascinating aspects of attachment relationships gone wrong. Sadly, these relationships are often mistaken by outsiders as strong attachment to the alienating parent and/or as lack of love and caring (or even fear of the relationship) with the targeted parent. With 50% of family structures involving divorce, education and awareness about how to understand healthy parent-child relationships becomes imperative to the welfare of our society's children.

Age of the child

While parental alienation can affect all children in a family, older children (e.g., ages 9-12) appear to be highly vulnerable.[1] Why this is the case is not entirely clear, but preadolescents and adolescents may be more vulnerable to distortions in reasoning and judgments, as well as to having an unquestioned allegiance with one of the parents. Likewise, they may have difficulties using critical thinking skills related to their families because they do not have a full understanding of the complexity of the problem. This situation also has potential consequences for their ability to view other life events and relationships with a realistic lens. As part of normal social development, children often split between parents, playing them off each other to get what they want. When such splitting occurs where there is parental alienation, conflict between the parents escalates and makes things worse all around.

Why are children susceptible to parental alienation tactics? Humans like to have consistency in their thoughts and behaviors, and when these are in conflict, they can feel great distress (a term referred to as *cognitive dissonance*[3]). Both parents are important for a child's identity, and when one parent criticizes or expresses hostility or negativity about the other parent that the child loves, the child begins to form two impressions, or *internal working models* of their alienating and targeted parents—one of a parent who is loving (perhaps based on actual experiences) and the second of a parent who is as bad as the alienating parent says they are. For a time, children can live with such disparate working models, but over time many (though not all) come to accept what is told to them, rather than what has actually transpired.

Young children in particular lack the ability to experience both negative and positive emotions towards the same person, and it is challenging for them to maintain an impartial perspective. Although older children and adolescents are more cognitively advanced and can potentially hold multiple perspectives for a time, they also may find it affectively easier to maintain one perspective (rather than multiple perspectives) of the same person. Many children cope by distancing themselves from the parent that is badmouthed.[4]

The impact of enmeshment

In a previous chapter, we discussed ways in which an alienating parent with features of a personality disorder (e.g., Borderline Personality Disorder) can affect the child, so we will not repeat those details here. Rather, we will focus on what happens in the context of an enmeshed parent-child dynamic with the alienating parent, what is really happening in a distanced relationship between the alienated parent and the child, and what healthy connections are actually like.

Many people believe that having a close connection between a parent and a child means they have a good relationship, and that a parent who is disconnected from their child is "bad" or not as good, even though the reasons for the disconnection may not be their fault. Unfortunately, this belief is false when a parent-child bond is *overly* connected in a way that excludes others in the family—these relationships are not good. It is also not a healthy relationship when the roles of parent and child become reversed, such as when a child feels responsible and protective of their parent's feelings and wants to take care of them. For example, one father we interviewed said that his son became anxious and pre-occupied with worry about his mother whenever she was demonstrating dramatic mood swings, which he knew were happening based on the tone of her email communications with him. As we described in an earlier chapter, researchers and theorists call these type of parent-child relationships as *insecure* or *dependent attachment*, or *enmeshed*.[2] Our research indicates that where there is parental alienation, one of the parent-child relationships tends to be "too close."

In many cases, the alienating parent has great need for their children, and when there are role-reversals with one of the children, this child takes on the spousal role to protect and calm their parent. They also are likely to take care of their siblings when the alienating parent "cannot." This situation is called *parentification* because the child essentially becomes the other parent in the new family system. Parentification often happens when a parent's own needs as a child were not met in their family of origin. Then, when they grow up and become parents themselves, they try to get their needs met through their children. The parentified child's needs are then not met and the cycle continues across multiple generations.[9]

Parentification is common when parental alienation is occurring. The parental alienator has a difficult time separating from the other parent when the relationship ends, and so the child takes their place. This replacement helps strengthen and intensify parental alienating behaviors against the ousted parent.[10] There is evidence that mothers are more likely to parentify than fathers,[11] and daughters are most often put into this unhealthy role than sons.[12]

Unfortunately, the child in this role is severely impacted. Developing healthy boundaries and a sense of autonomy is important for personal growth, and enmeshment with the parent stunts this important process. The parentified child oftentimes struggles with developing healthy peer and adult relationships, particularly with the other parent. These children become depressed, anxious, isolated, and even suicidal.[13] They also must comfort their alienating parent who is coping with the separation, and the cost is not being able to address their own grief.[11] We interviewed a number of targeted parents who expressed concern for their oldest children being parentified—many took on the role of taking care of younger children while the alienating parent was consumed with grief. These children were not able to just be kids.

Similar to parentification, *adultification* occurs when a child is made to be like a peer, or "best friend" to the alienating parent. This child has a partner-like, or allied relationship with the parent, and is made privy to many things that they are not mature enough to know, or should not even be made aware of due to their role as a child. For example, many targeted parents told us that their children spied on them and reported to the alienator on how much money they spent whenever they went out or bought groceries, and asked questions about changes to their job that would not have been known if their ex-spouse had not been stalking them on LinkedIn. These children are placed into a "partner in crime" role with the alienator that is very unhealthy.

Parents who adultify seek validation from their children because they lack support from others around them. According to Benjamin Garber, the children's eagerness to please the parent is misinterpreted as being "mature" and "insightful."[13] These children are typically the first born and appear mature on the surface but they are emotionally stunted. Adultified children often enjoy the status their parent gives them, however they are highly vulnerable to depression and other forms of psychological problems. We interviewed one father whose daughter was adultified; the alienating mother believed that at age 14, her daughter was a "mature teenager" and able to make her own mental health decisions about what psychologist she wanted to see and whether (or not) she wanted to ever see her father.

Finally, children who are enmeshed with an alienating parent can also be *infantilized*. In this case, the parent needs to feel needed; they thwart the child's healthy and appropriate need for autonomy and independence and are very overprotective of them. This parent may attempt to home-school or socially isolate the child. When the infantilized child is with the targeted parent, the alienator experiences loss, depression, anxiety, and other negative emotions, making the child not want to visit the targeted parent in order to protect the infantalizer. Children who are infantilized may still sleep or bathe with parents long after it is developmentally appropriate to do so. When both parents are interviewed, they may describe their children's behaviors very differently: in the home of the infantalizer, the child acts developmentally regressed as a way to garner approval from them (e.g. using baby talk when they are too old for this), while they act more age-appropriate in the other healthy parent's home.

Extreme cases of infantilizing may involve the parent having a Factitious Disorder by Proxy (formerly Munchausen by Proxy Syndrome), which is a form of child abuse where the parent exaggerates or fabricates illnesses in a child.[14] The parent then uses this illness as an excuse to restrict the child from seeing the other parent. For example, one of the fathers we interviewed said that the alienating mother reported being diagnosed with many fatal and chronic illnesses (e.g., cancer, multiple sclerosis) to get sympathy and more alimony. When these diagnoses could not be proven because there were no medical reports to support her claims, she then started a long campaign to make the children appear sick, mentally ill, and dependent so that she would have a reason to stay home to care for them (in other words, not have to work). Years after their divorce, this mother continued to report childhood illnesses that had long since resolved, shopped around for therapists and medical providers to give medications for the children for illnesses that had not been formally diagnosed (e.g., anxiety), and protested his travel with the children with false claims that he did not give their children the medication they needed.

Distancing from the targeted parent

When a child appears disconnected from a parent, this is often viewed as an insecure or *avoidant* attachment. There may be many reasons a child appears uncomfortable when they are with the targeted parent. One of us (Dr. Biringen) has developed a highly utilized system of evaluating parent-child interactions (The Emotional Availability (EA) Scales) and has been doing research for over 25 years on both assessing emotional availability and in ameliorating problems of emotional availability in parent-child relationships. The research process entails video recording parent-child interactions and looking for specific behaviors that show how emotionally connected the parents and children are with each other. Based on research conducted in approximately 30 cultures, she finds that a parent cannot look "good" without the child; if a child is cool and distant toward the parent, it is technically impossible for the parent to make the one-way street look beautiful—he or she needs the child to make it harmonious and satisfying. From an observer's point of view, this dynamic can be used--as an unfortunate error--against a targeted parent: it will appear the child does not care about that parent no matter what the targeted parent does.

Such relational avoidance may be due to the parent and child not having spent much quantity and quality time together. Indeed, many targeted parents we interviewed worked a lot prior to the divorce and had less contact with their children than the alienating parent. After their relationships ended, they struggled with having parenting time and this made repairing and maintaining a secure connection with their children difficult at best. Another reason for rejection is that the parent may have been abusive or neglectful of the child and the child is then rightfully estranged. While actual abuse and neglect might look like a parent and child are disconnected, research indicates that children may also appear close to their abusers, especially when the abuse is ongoing.[5] This phenomenon is similar to children who have been kidnapped and side with/speak fondly of their captors after the police are on the scene (also known as the Stockholm syndrome).[6]

We interviewed one mother who described how her relationship with her children changed once the alienating father moved into a new home several hours from where she lived. Her children were then isolated from her extended family and friends, and the father interfered with her being able to visit with the children. These children then started believing stories about their mother that were greatly exaggerated and untrue, and soon refused to even talk to her. Sadly, their grades at school plummeted and one of the children started abusing drugs. The father's isolation of the children resulted in serious psychological damage to them. Research on domestic violence indicates that when a woman becomes isolated from friends and family, she becomes more vulnerable to intimate partner violence.[7] Is it possible that when a child is isolated from the larger family system by a parental alienator, there is greater likelihood of abuse? Such isolation tactics are in and of themselves a form of emotional abuse, even when it appears the child wants it this way.

Many of our interviewees reported that what pains them the most about their situations was believing that their child or children are in the custody of a person who is manipulative and emotionally unhealthy, while they, the healthier parent, are ousted from the family system. Given how complex these relationship dynamics are, it behooves those who are making child custody recommendations to the courts to be well-versed in these relationship dynamics and how they affect parent-child attachments.

How can a healthy connection be understood?

In contrast to distant and/or overly close relationships, a child's healthy emotional connections in the family system (whether intact or divorced) involve a balance between feeling connected to their parents *and* feeling like they also have the freedom to explore the world around them. Children –at any age--who feel secure in a parent-child relationship become empowered by that relationship to freely explore the world, both in their thoughts and behaviors. Keeping one's children too close and not giving them the opportunity to explore and experience different attachment relationships in the family (both parents, extended family of both parents) seriously limits the children's ability to grow and flourish as human beings. This dependent attachment is often mistaken for a strong attachment, but a healthy, secure attachment is characterized by the freedom to explore and having a sense of agency and choice.

We believe that the theories psychologists use to understand the attachment between parents and children need to be revised when we are looking at divorced or separated families. For example, just being able to say negative things about a targeted parent and having it affect the child's attachment to them poses a serious problem for theories we have about attachment, because the actual parent-child interaction may be only a small contributor to how securely attached children become to parents when they are being alienated. Many of our interviewees stated that their alienated child accused them of abuse or other trauma that never occurred, and this affected their attachment to them. This issue is particularly problematic for fathers, who are often dependent on the good graces of the mother to form solid, secure attachments with their children.

Many times, attachment researchers assume that when a child is not securely attached to a parent, it is the parent's fault. While there is a moderate relationship between a parent's sensitivity to a child and his or her attachment,[8] we do not yet know how alienating behaviors affect these attachments. We interviewed one father who had a very close relationship with his teenage daughter prior to his divorce. After the divorce, his daughter cut off all communication with him due to believing lies that her mother told her about his having an affair. Ironically, the mother herself ran away with another man. When a mother badmouths the father, does this affect the child's attachment more to him than when the situation is reversed?

Such examples highlight how current theories we have about attachment cannot account for how positive relationships with one parent can turn sour so quickly. We are proposing a revision of attachment theory such that the perspective of each person in the relationship can be different: an alienated child can be avoidant and believe the targeted parent is despicable, while the targeted parent may have been loving and sensitive in their relationship—the attachment is influenced not only by the targeted parent's behaviors, but also by the words and stories said, and actions taken by the alienating parent in the family system.

The concept of *social referencing* is also important here. Social references are the people a child looks to when they are in need of guidance or security in an uncertain situation. Babies as young as 7-months of age will take cues from a parent's facial expressions about what to do;[9] if a situation feels uncertain and their mother looks scared, the child will be scared. Most research on social referencing has looked at mothers in two-parent

families and not with divorced families where allegiances
may be split. We believe that once the post-divorce family
system is established, a child will look to the dominant
member to take their cues. For example, the dominant
mother may agree to allow her kids to visit with the
father, but only if she is present. She may lurk in the
corner in order to "protect" her child from their loving
father. While these behaviors may seem extreme, they
were commonly described by the parents in our
interviews. What does the child learn from this type of
situation? That he or she needs protection from a
"demon" in their midst and the alienating parent is the
only one who can provide it.

Similarly, the *emotional availability* of one parent
toward the child is affected by the child's emotional
availability towards them. The traditional way of viewing
emotional availability is that it is a mutually rewarding
system: the parent's behaviors nurture the child's positive
behaviors, which then feed back into the parent's
behaviors. This cyclical description does not explain
relationships in the context of parental alienation where
the mutually rewarding system can be interrupted by what
the alienating parent does, says, or implies. In this case,
the targeted parent doesn't have to do anything-- the
words and deeds of the alienating parent have more

influence than what the targeted parent does. As a result, the relationship between the child and the targeted parent is not mutual or symmetrical; instead, it is influenced by the alienating parent.

What is often misunderstood is that even if a parent shows signs of being emotionally unavailable, their caregiving can be dramatically improved with short-term parenting classes. These classes teach parents skills to interact with a child who demonstrates these avoidant behaviors. For this to be successful, however, the parent who is being "rejected" by a child needs to have access to the child and enjoy some uninterrupted quality parenting time. Based on our combined clinical and research experience, we can assure you that a child's heart does not grow fonder with parental absence. Instead, the absence leaves a void and strong feelings of abandonment in the child, even when the child is fiercely adamant about that parent being poisonous or dangerous.

"Cumulative trauma" for children

The divorce process is traumatic for children in divorces where parental alienating behaviors are being played out.[11,12] In fact, we view the never-ending conflicts and hostilities, their lack of resolution, as well as the attachment disruptions that usually occur in such family systems as *cumulative trauma* for children. People often think of child abuse as the result of discrete and identifiable events, such as hitting a child and leaving a bruise. *In the case of parental alienation, however, child abuse involves a large number of behaviors exhibited over many years.* Therefore, this form of abuse is hard to identify unless one has the *entire* history of the family and knows what to look for. Children in such families often experience severe conflicts of loyalty that result in feelings of sadness, guilt, and depression, as well as the development of substance abuse disorders, and engagement in promiscuous sexual activity. Children also learn from the alienating parent how to be aggressive in relationships. For example, the greater amount of time that adolescent girls are exposed to family dysfunction, the more aggressive they are towards other girls (e.g., gossiping and bullying).[13]

Many alienated children develop what is called a "false self," which is an unauthentic self based on a desire to please the alienator and protect their true self from what is happening. When a child develops this false self, they appear on the surface to be better adjusted than they really are.[15] Further, Amy Baker reported lower levels of well-being in adults who believed they were alienated as children, including having lower self-esteem, greater guilt, anxiety, and depression, and lack of trust toward themselves and others.[16]

Although we did not interview children for this book, we do have reports from the targeted parents about how their children behaved and coped. There were many reports of conduct disorders, substance abuse once the children reached early and late adolescence, vandalism of property, self-mutilating behaviors (e.g., cutting), inability to form healthy romantic relationships as adults, and psychiatric symptoms such as depression and anxiety. Many children believed the false stories they were told about the targeted parent and were heavily medicated with drugs ranging from Ritalin to anti-anxiety and anti-depressant medications. Psychiatric symptoms such as anxiety and depression in children are often indicative of living (or having lived through) traumatic experiences. Such children are labeled as having a psychological problem when it is in fact the parental alienation in the family system that is creating cumulative trauma.

Some children are sensitive and suggestible to alienation tactics and become active participants in the alienation themselves. These children often experience great guilt (whether conscious or not) for their role in perpetuating the alienation and this can manifest in many ways, such as in psychosomatic symptoms like having frequent migraines and stomach aches that have no other identifiable cause. Children's outcomes also depend on what exactly they are being told about why the other loving parent should now be viewed as despicable. In one case, an alienating mother apparently told her first born daughter that she had been molested by her father when she was a child. The daughter was also told that the father abandoned them. Given this false information, the eldest broke off all ties to her father and to date has not replied to his emails for the three years she has been away at college. She also has not had any long-term or healthy romantic relationships. Fabricated stories about infidelity and abandonment create serious trauma in children and adolescents.

Where there is trauma, there is also
hope and resilience

Independent and critical thinking skills serve as important buffers for children from an alienating parent's tactics. For example, one young boy told his targeted parent, "I don't judge people by their words, but by their actions. I can think independently." We even heard one targeted step-mother recall her 4 year old step-daughter telling her son, "My mommy told me I should hate you and be mean to you, but I won't because I like you." Many children caught in the middle of unhealthy family dynamics employ critical thinking skills and are not easily swayed by the alienator. At the same time, they often need to hide what they truly believe about the targeted parent and new family members (e.g., step- or half-siblings) from the alienator. Expressing such positive sentiment for them often results in punishment or even ostracism. These children end up compartmentalizing their lives: they live as two different people when they are with the targeted and alienating parents. One parent described his now adult daughter (who reestablished contact) recalled having to live as two different personalities during her childhood. She acted as if she feared being in harm's way during visits with her dad in order to please her mother, but she really was not scared at all. The daughter thought that her dad knew she did not really feel that way about him, but he actually was only made aware of this fact after they redeveloped their relationship years later.

Sibling relationships are also impacted by parental alienation. Alienated children are pressured not to speak with siblings that were rejected by the alienator because they are perceived as having "sided" with the targeted parent. As a result, the alienated child often experiences grief not only for the targeted parent, but also for the loss of their sibling(s). However, some siblings attempt to "talk sense" into their alienated brothers and/or sisters by communicating with them about the targeted parent's side of the story with the hope that their sibling will start to be more critical of the alienator. For example, one half-sibling told the other, "Mom really loves you and she is trying her best to make this better....give her a chance." In some cases, this bonding of similar-aged siblings can be an important factor in improving relationships in the larger family system, and are a potential source of resilience.

We believe that those engaging in alienation strategies do so because they do not care to have a good relationship with the other parent and this ultimately results in damage to their children. Often, such damage is not visible because the alienating individual is not looking or does not want to see it. If they do notice negative impacts on the children, they often immediately blame then targeted parent and refuse to acknowledge their own role in the situation. When a child is told that the targeted parent is not interested in a relationship with and/or has abandoned him or her, this message deals a traumatic blow to their self-esteem, and many of them continue to blame themselves for their parent's separation or divorce well beyond their childhood years. Thus, the message to anyone considering or conducting alienation is to *consciously* back off and not transfer feelings onto others, particularly their children.

"Justifiable" alienation

It is important to state here that children who are actually abused find it very difficult to talk about such abuse. In contrast, children who are alienated want their parent(s) and everyone else (e.g., the courts, grandparents, friends) to know that they no longer want to see one parent. They are very free in their disdain, though it is difficult for them to describe specific incidents that contribute to their disdain.

Allegations of abuse need to be thoroughly investigated so that custody is not granted to a perpetrator. However, in the absence of substantiation, continued allegations of abuse and neglect should be stricken from all legal records and not be allowed to continuously taint and twist stories about the targeted parent. Courts need to operate on the basis (drawn from scientific evidence) that *both* parents have value in a child's life, unless one or both parents are deemed abusive or neglectful.

The effects of parental alienation on children are not trivial and are, in fact, very traumatic. But how does it impact others such as the targeted parent, their extended family members, and society? We turn to these questions next.

CHAPTER SEVEN

HOW DOES ALIENATION IMPACT THE TARGETED PARENT, FAMILY, AND COMMUNITY?

Any parent married to or in a relationship with someone who has the traits of an alienator is vulnerable to parental alienation. Like domestic violence, this problem does not affect one group more than another. It cuts across all socio-economic groups, races, and nationalities. The consequences of parental alienation for these parents are substantial and devastating, and the parent is often left with little recourse other than to seek help from legal and mental health professionals. Many parents give up trying to constantly repair their relationship with their hostile child, whether due to lack of financial support, concerns that fighting in the courts will be too costly or emotionally traumatic for the child, or because they lack the energy or psychological wherewithal to continuously try.[1]

Across both targeted mothers and fathers, feelings of powerlessness and frustration are common;[2] indeed, many parents are told that they have "no chance" to fight the alienation in court because they will never win, particularly fathers. Many fall into depression, experience repeated trauma, and are diagnosed with Posttraumatic Stress Disorder (PTSD). For example, one highly successful father we talked to shared feelings of immense stress whenever he received a text from his ex-wife. This successful businessman had to learn mindfulness meditation and stress relaxation techniques that he practiced before and after reading these texts. Otherwise, he was unable to function at work.

Coping with parental alienation was reported by all the parents we interviewed as being extremely time consuming; for many it was like a full-time job. Most parents spent in excess of 20-30 hours a week preparing for court and thinking with worry and longing for their children nearly all day long. The majority of parents we spoke with reported having problems sleeping. Many had to regularly take time off from work to attend court hearings and meetings with attorneys. As a result, a large number of them lost their jobs.

Aside from the time parental alienation consumed, fighting for rights to see their children in the courts was financially devastating for everyone we spoke with. Christine Giancarlo and Kara Rottman found in interviews they conducted with targeted parents that 79% lost their homes because of being unable to pay the mortgage or rent, having had a lien placed on their home by their lawyer, being in arrears for child support payments, or losing their job.[3] We spoke with a large number of targeted parents who had lost their homes and had to move in with extended family due to their legal expenses. Mothers and fathers oftentimes spent their entire life savings and owed substantial legal debts, ranging from \$50,000 to \$80,000 or more. Several wealthy fathers we interviewed reported spending over \$1 million on legal expenses, only to be awarded partial visitation that they were rarely able to enforce. One such father we interviewed had relocated to a foreign country where his son was residing with his mother and still had not seen his son for over two years. These parents wondered aloud how parents with less means had any chance to fight for their rights to have a relationship with their children.

The pain, grief and stress caused by being the target of parental alienation makes parenting of children difficult to do effectively.[4] In the best of times, it is hard to be emotionally present and understanding with a child who is hostile and negative towards you. One father we spoke with described how his children destroyed his home whenever they came to visit. His son destroyed the plumbing in the home by pouring things down the drain, and his daughter smashed many holes in the walls. He later discovered that his children were being rewarded by their mother for doing these behaviors. He started meeting with his children only in public places to prevent further damage to his house, but then his children started yelling and screaming at him in front of others. It got to the point that he decided to let the children decide whether they wanted to visit him or not. He had not seen them in over 7 years at the time of our interview.

Parents can also become passive and withdrawn from their children, hoping that this will stop the behavior of the alienating parent. This approach rarely works. They may also develop less and less empathy for the child and become critical, harsh or rigid in their parenting style as a way to control their insolent and hostile behaviors.[5] Some parents were not willing to admit to others that they even have children because it was too hard and painful to explain to co-workers and friends why their children could not, or did not want to spend time with them. They also did not want to burden people with the drama that was hard and oftentimes too complicated to explain. The impact alienation has on parenting ability lends support to Janet Johnston's argument that rejected parents can perpetuate the alienation inadvertantly;[6] it is a lose-lose situation for them.

While the impact of parental alienation on targeted parents was quite similar across mothers and fathers in our interviews, we did notice some differences in how alienation was accomplished, which had a direct impact on how they coped. In this next section, we will briefly review some of the different strategies and coping responses. It is important to mention that there were some mothers and fathers whose experience resembled those of the other gender. We will only present overall patterns we saw across all of the interviews and then explore why these differences exist in subsequent chapters.

Effects on the fathers

The majority of parental alienation targets are non-custodial fathers, and there has been little research attention directed at how they cope with their strained and severely restricted relationships with their children. The most common themes that came out of our interviews which were somewhat unique for fathers were:

(1) allegations of sexual or physical abuse and stated fear of the father by one or more children, even when there were no documented incidents or substantiating evidence;

(2) allegations of domestic violence towards the mother (oftentimes a single incident) where the

police were called but no evidence was present of actual abuse;

(3) an overscheduling of the children in activities during the father's parenting time and without regard for the divorce decree, leading to nearly complete lack of access to the children for months or even years;

(4) use of disparaging or objectifying language in front of the children (e.g., 'he' is coming; you'll need to go see 'him') over a period of time that makes the children fearful of contact with the father; and

(5) spreading lies to anyone who will listen (children, teachers, neighbors) that make the father appear dangerous.

The impact? Trauma—pure and simple. The fathers we interviewed cried, both openly and silently, about losing their children. Many were worried their children would develop similar mental health issues as their mother. This trauma affected the fathers' psychological well-being, work productivity, economic stability, and even their new relationships. Theories of post-divorce parenting indicate that a father's emotional and material well-being shapes their fathering capacities and ability to parent.[7] Unfortunately, because many fathers struggled with trauma, their limited time with their children was not high quality. As a result, the children may perceive their father as incapable of being loving due to his emotional and financial strains, and this further aligns them with the alienator.

Social support is one of the most important sources of coping when going through painful life events, and the targeted fathers we spoke to often lacked this. Many of the fathers said they felt relief having finally shared their story with us because we understood what parental alienation is and they did not have to spend time explaining themselves. Too often, they reported, people either did not understand, or did not care enough to even try and understand what they were going through. For some, their only support was a new romantic or marital partner, but entering these relationships oftentimes intensified the alienation.

One father reported that his second marriage failed because he had to spend all his money and time fighting to even see his children because his ex-wife stopped visitation once he got married. Another father started a local Meetup.com group that had over 30 members join within the first week. At their first meeting, he discovered that most of the members were step-mothers trying to get support for their alienated husbands. Seeking support is not as consistent with the male gender role as it is for females, so many men suffer alone and in silence. The grief of loss was so extreme in some cases that some fathers reported wishing their children had died-- not being able to have a relationship with them while they were alive was a form of unresolvable grief. Several targeted fathers we spoke to had attempted suicide in the past and reported knowing many others who had been successful.

Disciplining was also challenging for many targeted fathers we interviewed because they constantly feared that their child or the alienating mother would report any form of discipline as abuse to the courts or mandatory reporters such as doctors and school counselors. Several fathers we spoke with even feared sending their children to their rooms for "time out," as it sometimes resulted in their children calling the police with claims of being abused. This constant fear of false allegations undermines many of these fathers' authority with their children and leaves them feeling emasculated. Even protecting oneself legally from the alienator's tactics demands self-control, patience, and planning; all characteristics that are difficult to use when one is traumatized and distressed.

There were some indicators of healthy coping among fathers. Some were able to form or maintain healthy relationships with one or more of their children. These relationships provided solace when they were sad about the loss of their other alienated children. Other parents sought out help on social media sites and local support groups, became advocates for law reform, and tried to mobilize and increase awareness of parental alienation among the general population. One father we interviewed had even returned to law school so that he could help other fathers fight for their children in family court.

Effects on the mothers

Our findings indicate that the effects of parental alienation on the mothers were very similar to how fathers were impacted, although they typically still had partial or full custody, or they still had regular or largely uninterrupted visits with their children. Having greater contact with their children resulted in less severe of an impact on the mother-child relationship, but this did not necessarily mean that it lowered the severity of the alienation strategies employed by the father or step-mother towards her. One mother we interviewed was able to partially repair her relationship with her daughter due to still having 50% custody, but she explained that her daughter was used as a weapon (even though it was not her fault) for many years. As a result, she reported not being able to trust her daughter and has found it hard to go back to having a loving relationship with a "weapon."

Despite inviting many mothers to participate in our study, there were many more fathers who completed our survey and agreed to be interviewed. Our research team has pondered many reasons for this, such as whether it is a reflection of actual gender differences in who is targeted, or because many women do not want to come forward out of shame or trauma at having her mother role stripped away, a role that is highly valued across cultures.[8] Among the mothers who did come forward, we heard about similar social and legal injustices that fathers experienced, and of being falsely condemned for exhibiting poor parenting practices. We saw several other themes that were somewhat unique for mothers:

(1) there was a dominant, affluent father (or affluent new family) with evidence of a personality disorder (typically narcissistic) who also had resources to distance the mother through the court system;

2) the mother was the "breadwinner" and the father was in the child caretaker role. This role reversal was often used against the mother to

demonstrate she was not as "motherly" as she should be, particularly if she was in a job where women are not well represented (e.g., engineering);

(3) allegations of being an unfit parent due to mental illness, abuse, and/or neglect; and

(4) having a child or children explicitly indicating or testifying in court or stating to a mental health professional that they clearly do not want to have any further contact with the mother.

Being labeled an ineffective or unfit parent is devastating, and for many women this is particularly true given the social value (and power) derived from the mother role. Although we found it was harder for fathers to get mental health and court officials to pin the "unfit mother" label onto mothers due to strong cultural stereotypes about them being better parents than fathers, this label was hard to shake for many mothers once it was assigned. Many personality and psychological disorders are more common among women than men, and some have more negative associations with being able to function as a parent than others. For example, a mother who has borderline personality disorder is not likely to ever be diagnosed, and being overly-caring and enmeshed with a child is consistent with the mother role (e.g., "she is being a good, concerned mother"). Other disorders such as depression, however, make mothers with this mental illness more vulnerable to parental alienation because she is then often accused of being neglectful of her children's needs.

Several mothers we spoke with reported experiencing anxiety attacks whenever their phone rang because there was always "bad news" related to their custody battle on the other end of the line. A large number of these mothers were on anti-depressants because they were so overwhelmed with grief and loss. Although many targeted fathers expressed having the same feelings, the mothers we interviewed often had these feelings used against them in court when they fought for custody or enforcement of parenting time, largely because the mental illness label was more stigmatizing for them than for the fathers. For example, one mother we interviewed reported being called "crazy" and too depressed and overwhelmed to care for her children by her ex-husband who was a medical provider. Her ex-husband had convinced many others to believe his clinical (albeit not objective) opinion. This campaign, achievable because of his expertise and status, allowed him to get custody of their children and he nearly blocked her access to them entirely.

Impact on step-parents

Step-parents are often targets of parental alienation because the alienator may feel very threatened by their role and relationship with the children. One targeted step-mother described to us how her 4 year old step-daughter told her about a Smart Phone app that lets people make monster faces using pictures saved on the phone. The step-daughter said that she was making lots of monster faces of her on her mother's phone-- in other words, the mother had somehow saved pictures of the step-mother on her phone and then encouraged her daughter to make her step-mother into a monster. Actions such as these make the child learn to dislike the step-parent, and they also serve to enhance the existing bond with the alienating parent.

Children may also feel resentment and jealousy towards the step-parent and their relationship with the mother or father.[9] Although Richard Gardner recommended that child custody evaluators consider the strength and nature of the bond between the child and step-parents, they also need to be sensitive to loyalty conflicts in the children. Many children play off their parents to get what they want and may say they dislike a step-parent to gain favor, even though they may really think the step-parent is nice or lovable.

We interviewed many step-mothers who were targeted by the mothers of their step-children. The tactics used were very similar to those used against the fathers, but the step-mothers often felt they had little power in the situation to do anything about the matter. Their rights to the step-children were even fewer than the fathers, and they oftentimes had to provide support to their husbands who were struggling to even communicate with their children. These step-parents had little support for their own feelings of trauma. While we interviewed a few targeted mothers who were remarried, we did not hear as many stories of how the step-fathers were targeted (and to what extent) or how they coped with it. Indeed, of all the targeted parents who completed our initial survey, only 1 of 28 step-parents was a step-father. We hope to explore this more as our work continues.

Do targeted parents retaliate?

Across our interviews, we asked all targeted parents whether they ever found themselves engaging in behaviors with their children that might be construed as alienating of the other parent. One response we heard frequently was that the parents had almost no time with their children to even have had the chance to alienate in retaliation. Even if they did have time, these parents said they would *never* say anything bad about the other parent, despite all the things that had been said about or done to them. These parents often explained quite eloquently that they understood how it impacted the child because of having done a considerable amount of research on the topic of alienation as a way to cope with their predicament. Many were well versed in all the research findings we have outlined in this book, and were very active in legal reform movements.

Some parents admitted to doing "stupid" things or making occasional disparaging remarks to their children about the other parent. The parents who acknowledged this behavior rarely provided specific details, which can either mean that the parent has a hard time sharing their negative experience generally, or that they are trying to minimize their role in the situation. Upon re-examination of the transcripts from the interviews with these parents, we came to the conclusion that most were disorganized in how they described their general experiences, which is a sign of trauma. It is possible they were very active participants in the alienation, but given the details provided in their interviews about what they were living through related to false allegations and other events, we came to the conclusion that this was unlikely.

Some parents admitted to doing specific things that were potentially alienating, but when compared to the definition of what parental alienating behaviors are, they were not. For example, one father discovered that his daughters regularly came to his home for weekend visits with cell phones sent by their mother. Their mother texted them constantly during their time with him. During one visit, he restricted use of the phone to one call per day to their mother, explaining that he wanted to enjoy uninterrupted time together with them. This father believed his action could be interpreted as alienation, however the mother's interference was itself the alienating behavior. Therefore, many parents were overly cautious of their behaviors to the point that they even interpreted protection of their time with their children as being alienating towards the other parent. This may be one way to distinguish between the alienating parent and the target; the alienator will not see anything wrong with interfering with the other parent's time, and will see all contact the targeted parent has with the children during their parenting time as "too much."

Given the many incentives parents have for alienating their children, ranging from personal, to financial, and legal, why do some parents *not* retaliate and alienate their children from the other parent? Nearly all of the reasons for not doing so appear to lie with the *value system of the parent*. Many of our interviewees said that they would not distance or alienate their children because they firmly believe it is important for the children to get to know and continue to know *both* parents, warts and all. A child is half of both parents; taking away one half leads to mystery about who they are and feelings of not being lovable themselves.

Other interviewees reported to us that they believe in egalitarian relationships. Such a value system appeared to be born of an evolved sense of self where the parent is not interested in manipulating the other parent or the system to satisfy their own selfish needs. These same parents could see that egalitarian ideals were just that -- ideals rather than reality, because the alienator was more dominant in wielding their influence in the marriage and with the children. Most of our interviewees had court ordered parenting plans that were egalitarian with respect to parenting time, but were not enforced by the legal system.

It is certainly possible that our sample of targeted parents differs from others in that there may actually be a number of targeted parents who retaliate and reciprocate the alienating parent's behaviors. It is also likely that many say things about the other parent that are disparaging and they have no idea that it has an effect on the child(ren). Indeed, in a prior study conducted by one of us (Biringen), some college students from both intact and divorced families recalled both parents as being alienators.[10] More research will need to be conducted to determine the frequency with which this dynamic occurs, and the impact it has on the targeted parents and children.

Impact on extended family

Extended family are also participants and victims of parental alienation. As we explained in an earlier chapter, we had many grandparents and extended family members (e.g., aunts) contact us to participate in our study because they were excluded from the children's lives by a parent. Many extended family members are roped into the campaign of an alienator to exclude the targeted parent and they actively work to push and erase the other parent from the children's lives. We heard numerous stories of grandparents attending children's sporting events and yelling at the targeted parent for simply being there, right in front of the children.

Whether the grandparents or extended family are alienators, or are simply victims of the alienator's propaganda is an interesting avenue for future research. More research also needs to be conducted to examine how the extended family of the targeted parent copes with the loss of the children. Some targeted parents described that holidays were particularly painful, as they often could not bring their children with them to family celebrations. Many could not even call or get in contact with their children on holidays, and this was very hard to explain to family members.

Impact on social networks

Friends of targeted parents are also impacted by alienation. We discovered in our interviews that many friends were used to push the targeted parent further out of the children's lives. Jointly held friends often sided with the alienator, either because of lies told to them about the targeted parent, or because their spouse was aligned with them and they could not split their allegiances. One mother we spoke to explained that her best friend from high school married her ex-husband soon after they divorced. The alienation only began after this happened and the new step-mother wanted to erase her from her children's lives. She lost not only her best friend, but all of the friends they shared in their social network. Many parents described not being able to get much support from friends because they often did not understand, or were too tired of hearing about their struggles. When they did stand up for the targeted parent, some friends were then targeted by the alienator as well. The amount of grief that targeted parents must endure is exceptional, and their friends also often take a toll.

We heard of many targeted parents who struggled to organize playdates or birthday parties for their children because their friend's parents had been told negative things about them. A father we interviewed described how pained his daughter was that only two of 15 girls invited to her birthday party attended; one mother even admitted to him that she was uncomfortable allowing her daughter to attend the party because of what the mother had said about him. Another mother we interviewed had a hard time explaining to the mother of her son's friend that she only had him for visits every other weekend. During their playdates, her son often spoke to her disrespectfully (as modelled by the alienating father), and this resulted in the friend's mother no longer inviting them over. Ultimately, the alienating parent's influence on friends further serves to isolate the targeted parent. The children also associate the negativity they perceive from these adults as social proof that their parent is dangerous or inadequate, and this further aligns them with the alienator.

Many alienating parents also enlist the help of neighbors, teachers, coaches, and others who are involved in the children's lives to distance the child from the targeted parent. While these individuals often mean well, they typically do not have enough exposure to the children and *both* parents to form an unbiased opinion about the situation. Sadly, many of these individuals are often asked to testify in court against the targeted parent, and their opinions (rather than objective observations) are weighed heavily in court decisions. For example, one mother we talked to explained how her ex-husband had a neighbor testify in court that she never fed her children. Her testimony carried considerable weight in a judge's determination that she was neglectful, despite her children having healthy body-mass-indices and no other objective signs of abuse.

Although many school officials and personnel do not like to get involved with child custody disputes, they are eventually pulled into the conflict. For example, many parental exchanges are ordered to take place at school, problems arise in interpreting what educational rights or decision-making mean for one or both parents, and staff sometimes have difficulties determining who to call when there is an emergency or medical issue with a child. School officials are sometimes manipulated to believe the alienator's interpretation of court orders and they restrict parental rights when they should not. For example, a father we interviewed was ordered visits with his daughter on a certain day of the week. One day, the mother informed the school that he was not allowed to pick his daughter up without her permission (which was not true according to the court order). The school administrators believed the mother, and would not release the child to the father when he went to the school to pick her up. He had to contact the police to help and faced considerable resistance from them to intervene because police do not typically want to get involved with domestic or civil matters. His child then was distressed about needing to have the police involved to see her father, and this created further alignment with the alienator.

One step-mother explained to us that her step-daughter's emergency contact information was continuously changed in her school records by the alienating mother. She was taken off her step-daughter's record multiple times each year and replaced with the names of family members who lived thousands of miles from the school. Each time she communicated this problem with the school, she felt they were somewhat sympathetic, but they never did anything because she was just a step-mother, not the *real* mother. Another step-mother reported to us that the alienating mother emailed a school administrator (with her cc'd) and asked that the step-mother not be included on any future email correspondence because she was just a "mistress" that the father later married (which was not true). Therefore, although schools and extracurricular activities can potentially offer a safe, neutral place for the child to be buffered from the alienation, the alienator often exerts their influence there in order to extend their destructive aggression beyond the immediate family.

Impact on the legal system

Family court systems are overburdened with parental alienation cases because legal interventions are often the only recourse that targeted parents have to enforce court ordered parenting time and to address the conflict they are experiencing. In 2012, for example, 647,475 family court cases were heard in New York State alone.[10] Such high caseloads result in lengthy wait times for hearings and it can often take over a year to even get a hearing with a judge to enforce court ordered parenting time. If an alienating parent is found to be in contempt of a court's orders, it can take many more months to schedule a hearing to apply sanctions, if the court does so at all.

Many parents and professionals working with divorce cases believe that the social work and legal systems support alienating parents and allow them to continuously get away with their damaging behaviors[11] because there is financial incentive to do so. Indeed, lawyers representing alienators continuously delay litigation and court proceedings involving changes to parenting plans or contempt of court for parenting plan violations (e.g., obstructing parenting time) for months or even years.[4] These delays give the alienating parent more one-on-one time with the children to work their damage. Some parents we interviewed reported that the alienating parent's lawyers use "tactical litigation strategies" to bombard and harass them with court motions, emails, and letters. Many parents even said that if the courts and lawyers had not been involved, no alienation would be occurring—*they believed there is a conspiracy to promote alienation in order to generate money.*

We heard of several cases in which the targeted parents tried to demonstrate that parental alienation was occurring by using expert testimony from mental health professionals (e.g., psychologists working with the children). Due to the fact that many courts have not yet recognized parental alienation as being a real phenomenon, these experts are often scrutinized and discredited by the alienating parent's lawyers. The targeted parent is then left with little defense against this abuse.

We interviewed numerous fathers who were falsely accused of sexually abusing their children and were encouraged by their lawyers to admit to doing it. Others were told to accept *any* parenting arrangement that was offered by the mother because there was little hope of aspiring to equal parenting time. Luckily, one of our interviewed fathers would not under any circumstance admit to the molestation of his children, given that he was not only innocent but also because he was a highly visible professional whose career would be ruined by such a false admission.

Many targeted parents report that legal professionals do not fully understand parental alienation, particularly the fact that it does not stop or go away as a child gets older and the separation/divorce is long over.[4] In fact, many stated that the advice from some of their legal professionals was either not helpful or completely erroneous. Christine Giancarlo and Kara Rottman have found that many lawyers and judges involved with parental alienation cases do not come prepared for court, they refuse to enter or challenge affidavits provided in defense of the targeted parent, they allow hearsay evidence, do not prosecute perjury, and they allow unethical practices such as only allowing the alienating parent to present witnesses and prohibiting the targeted parent from cross-examination.[3] These parents and their children are abused by a system that is supposed to protect them. Most parents we spoke with lost complete faith that there was such a thing as justice in family court.

Further, courts have become too comfortable with allowing parents to "act badly," and many rely heavily on custody evaluations that rarely include information about parental personality disorders or such features that may impact parenting capabilities. There is also a tendency for the courts to say "just work it out," as if blame for the conflict between parents should be shared equally, when in fact only one of the parents may be significantly distorting history and/or everyday facts. There is also a tendency for courts to issue empty threats, rather than any sanctions "with teeth" when a parent breaks the law about providing access to the children, per the court's decree. Courts also do not seem inclined to use scientific information on child development—although the term "attachment" is used by mental health and legal professionals alike, the usage bears little resemblance to how psychological and family studies researchers define attachment. Children need appropriate love and caring, not distance, enmeshment, or apparent abandonment. Finally, courts do not often take a "relationship" perspective on what is in "best interests of the child,"-- relationships are at the heart of all aspects of child development, and giving children the right to choose which parent they prefer makes alienation institutionally sanctioned and distances children from their loving families.

In summary, *we believe that parental alienation is a form of unrecognized trauma for the targeted parents* and *for the children whose attachments become disrupted.* It also negatively impacts extended family, friends, school systems, and other social structures. Now that we have explored how parental alienation affects children and those around them, we are still left with questions regarding why this such a problem today. How do alienators get away with this? Why do we (neighbors, friends, extended family, the schools, the courts) continue to stand by and let them get away with the pain and chaos they create? How do cultural changes and institutions enable this behavior and create a problem that has reached epidemic proportions? We now turn to these questions.

CHAPTER EIGHT

HOW DO PARENTAL ROLES, GENDER, AND POWER CONTRIBUTE TO PARENTAL ALIENATION?

Parental alienation has no doubt been occurring for many, many generations. Today it appears to be at epidemic levels, worldwide. How have things gotten so bad? Despite many clinical and legal interventions, the problem is not going away. Finding effective solutions to the problem involves an identification of why it came to be, and then an understanding of how cultural and institutional contexts are impacting what is happening. To start, let's begin with an examination of parental roles and how they have changed over time. Our review here is not exhaustive or detailed, and we know summaries gloss over and overlook many nuances. For our purposes, however, we do need to provide a general overview of the societal, cultural, and legal influences that bring the current state of the problem into focus.

Parenting and the family

There has been considerable debate within the field of anthropology over the role of the father in the family.[1] In many animal species, a male's role in raising offspring is limited to reproduction or protection of territory. Across human cultures, families have been important because we have an extended period of childhood and adolescence, and we are socialized into more complex cultures compared to other animals.

Mothering and fathering behaviors are actually very similar; men generally engage in less direct physical care (e.g., feeding), but engage in more active play than mothers. For example, American fathers hold infants more, engage in more physical play with their children, stimulate them more than mothers, and hold them so that they are facing the world, while mothers engage in more verbal play and hold infants facing them instead of the outside world. Mothers and fathers also show more affection with children of the opposite sex, and more arousal and play with children of the same sex. *Both parent's roles in the family are important for a child's development.*

In many "traditional" societies (for lack of a better word), it is not unmanly for fathers to show affection towards infants, and fathers play with their children for considerable lengths of time each day (sometimes around 13-14% of the day). Until industrialization, boys worked regularly alongside their fathers or other adult male figures as apprentices, and fathers were protectors and educators even in their most limited roles. Despite having strong bonds with their mothers, children also have firm and strong feelings of emotional security and attachment bonds with their fathers. For example, both Bushmen and Yanomami girls and boys protest when their father leaves for work or to hunt, even if their mother stays home.[1]

While gender differences in parenting behaviors are actually quite small across cultures, *expectations* for how mothers and fathers are supposed to act have varied considerably across time and place. These cultural differences are due largely to how humans structure themselves in society along gender lines.

Patriarchy, parenthood, and "best interests of the child"

Jim Sidanius and Felicia Pratto, two social psychologists who developed social dominance theory, one of the most widely tested theories of oppression and discrimination, have observed that humans organize themselves in several set ways, gender being one of them. Importantly, there has been no known society in which women as a group have had more social and political power in their communities than men. There are a few matriarchal cultures and groups where material wealth and other resources are passed along the maternal side of families, however there are no known societies where women as a group have had more power than men.[2] Does this mean women are powerless? No. We will get to where and how power is used in relationships shortly, but let us first describe what patriarchy is and how it has impacted parenting role expectations.

There are many definitions of patriarchy, but it essentially means social or cultural systems in which men have more access and ability to use power and resources than women, and this allows for women to be dominated, oppressed and exploitated.[20] Some early definitions stated that men exert their power through their role as head of households, but this has been extended to other domains like work and education. Patriarchy impacts our expectations for the roles that mothers and fathers have in families. For example, in ancient Rome, the eldest male was head of household and had complete control over all family members; this meant he also had the "right" to kill any of his children[3] because he had the right to unmake what he had originally made. Although this right was rarely exercised and was later restricted by law, the culture at the time supported the idea that a man was not expected to make decisions for the benefit of family, necessarily, but rather for himself.

This father-as-overseer role persisted well into the eighteenth and early nineteenth centuries; fathers provided moral teaching and "worldly" judgment because they were perceived as having more superior reasoning than mothers. Rarely were parental expectations explicitly provided for mothers. Under English law, which was also applied in the U.S. and many other countries until the late 1800s, fathers were granted primary custody of children when they divorced because they were their "property."[4] Ludwig Lowenstein has argued that father alienators were more common in times when they had "supreme power over families and children" and that this power was often misused (p. 662).[5]

With industrialization in the early nineteenth and mid-twentieth centuries in many parts of the world, men worked farther from the home for more extended lengths of time. Except for brief periods of time when women were needed in the workplace while men were away at war (e.g., World War II), women's role as mother and child care provider became more and more valued by society. The mother role was now a more important parent than the father role, as fathers were expected to be the primary breadwinners.[6] Mothers were perceived as "pure" and the domestic world "belonged" to her. Dr. Spock's advice books on how to raise children, popular in the early to mid-20th century, exemplifies the portrayal of the selfless mother who was expected to stay at home while the father worked.[7]

Child custody after divorce or separation at this time was often granted to mothers due to these changes in role expectations.[6] In the late 1800s, mothers and fathers were *both* able to get custody of the children after divorce, but mothers were now starting to be seen as the ideal parent for raising psychologically healthy children and the preference for custodial status started leaning in her direction. Indeed, psychological theories popular in the early 1900s (e.g., psychodynamic theories) and beyond promoted the mother-child relationship as primary, and fathers as less involved and important. This perspective led to what is known as the *tender years doctrine* employed in many child custody determinations; young children were perceived as needing the mother's love for healthy development more than the father's.

In summary, while primary custody of children was often given to fathers at a time when "father knows best," it shifted to mothers having primary custody because they were viewed as being better at parenting than them. Indeed, much of the 1900s entailed custody being assigned to mothers 90% of the time,[8] and this is one reason why there are distinct gender differences in who alienates today. The custodial parent is typically the alienator, and because mothers most often have more custody, they are more likely to alienate than fathers. While most mothers today would not likely follow up on the threat, "I brought you into this world, and I can take you out of it," such common statements reflect the power that mothers today have over children in their domestic role, which was a role occupied by fathers at another time in history when they were more likely to be alienators.

Egalitarianism

During the civil rights era of the 1960-70s in the United States, egalitarianism, or equal rights for men and women, started to become a widely endorsed social value. This cultural shift was occurring in many other parts of the world as well, particularly in Western Europe. Women entered the workforce in greater numbers and men started to buck traditional gender roles to be more available as fathers. Harry Chapin's classic song "Cats in the cradle" highlighted a growing dissatisfaction with the "unavailable" father stereotype:

> *I've long since retired, my son's moved away*
> *I called him up just the other day*
> *I said, "I'd like to see you if you don't mind"*
> *He said, "I'd love to, Dad, if I can find the time*
> *You see my new job's a hassle and kids have the flu*
> *But it's sure nice talking to you, Dad*
> *It's been sure nice talking to you"*
> *And as I hung up the phone it occurred to me*

He'd grown up just like me
My boy was just like me
And the cat's in the cradle and the silver spoon
Little boy blue and the man on the moon
When you comin' home son?
I don't know when, but we'll get together then son
You know we'll have a good time then.[9]

The men's movement brought to the forefront many other challenges to fatherhood and male stereotypes, such as with the book *Iron John: A Book about Men* by Robert Bly. This book highlights how fathers, who are expected to be the breadwinners, are often absent due to having to work long hours to support their families. The result? A generation of young boys is raised who do not have formal rites of passage to become men and fathers of the world. According to Bly, becoming a man in the U.S. today means rejecting one's father because fathers are not admirable anymore. This rejection of fathers results in a lack of confidence and ability to be generous with others, and it extends to all men in American society; few rely on each other or feel obligated to mentor and nurture young men. Instead, they compete with each other.[10]

At this same time, psychologists started acknowledging the important role fathers have in children's development. A father's active involvement now was viewed by some as being important not because mothers are inadequate, but because fathers can also make a valuable contribution to the well-being of children and families.[11] These challenges to traditional gender and parenting stereotypes in the 1960s and 1970s resulted in normative changes across the U.S. and other Westernized countries. Children who grew up at this time had mothers who wanted to work to support their family because they were just as capable in the workplace as fathers. It is easier (and arguably more necessary due to economic reasons) for mothers to work today than in the past. These children's fathers wanted to be more involved and connected to their children. Young men growing up in this generation learned that fathers should not be absent or "deadbeats," as this was a stereotype they longed to reject. Boys raised at this time in history are more likely to be stay-at home parents today than the generation before them: nearly 2 million fathers stay at home while their wives work today, a statistic that has doubled since 1989.[12]

Despite changes in psychological opinion in the latter part of the 20th century about the importance of fathers for children's development, a number of psychologists also thought that if the child had one primary custodial parent and a continuous relationship with another one, conflict would result.[13] The *best interest of the child* principle is something that has been applied by judges and magistrates when the courts are trying to determine what decision will serve a child's needs the best. Many clinicians working with divorced families believe that because of how best interests of the child has changed in response to psychological research showing that fathers are important, fathers have started to get more paternal rights and time with their children. The result, in their opinion, is that parental alienation has increased.[14] Indeed, Richard Gardner argued that the rise in child custody disputes started in the 1970s due to the change from the "tender years" to the "best interests of the child" principle. He also believed that this increase occurred because courts were asked to ignore gender in assigning custody.

Additionally, the concept of joint custody also began to erode the primary caregiving status of mothers after divorce, leading to more intense custody battles than ever before. Recommendations to family court judges were to go with the *least detrimental alternative* in their custody decisions, which was very subjective in its application. In 1957, North Carolina was the first state in the U.S. to institute a joint custody statute, and other states soon followed. This custody arrangement was recommended when couples were deemed able to co-parent, had the ability to compromise, and had little conflict.[13] Unfortunately, these types of separations are uncommon, and many states that adopted similar statutes have interpreted "joint" custody very differently. Clinicians also disagreed as to whether such arrangements were beneficial for children's outcomes, and even suggested it was worse for younger than older children.

By the mid-1990s, a number of legal and clinical professionals argued that the best interest of the child principle should be changed to *best interest of the family.*[4] This fundamental shift in perspective prompted a change in how families were then (supposed to be) evaluated for custody recommendations. Although legal interventions such as mediation have had promise in creating more positive outcomes between parents in child custody disputes than family court (e.g., improved communication, cooperation), they have not demonstrated better effects for children. The only factor that really improves outcomes for children is reduced parental conflict. Therefore, while family courts have attempted to address parental alienating behaviors by instituting particular custody arrangements and using alternative legal interventions, *this is not effective when a parent is an alienator.*

Egalitarianism brought about the promise of greater structural gender equality and changes to parental role expectations, however it is also one of the underlying reasons why we are seeing such high levels of parental alienation today. It is also why mothers and fathers are able to use different strategies to effectively accomplish their alienation campaigns. This is all linked to power.

Power derived from the parental role

When we asked parents what they think motivates the alienator's behavior, we heard time and again that it is all about power and control. But what is power and how is it expressed in cases of parental alienation? There is no agreement among social scientists about what exactly power is. Some define power as a feeling of agency, or having the personal, social, or political resources to influence or control others (whether one acts on it or not).[15] Others consider power as being something that comes out of specific relationship dynamics--for example, a person who is more dependent on their partner has less influence on them.[16]

Felicia Pratto and her colleagues have argued that power arises out of basic human needs.[17] For example, we all have needs for wholeness (e.g., being psychologically and physically healthy), to feel care and love from other people, and to reproduce. Each of these needs results in a different type of power. For example, resource consumption needs (e.g., eating) results in power to control resources. Needing to feel cared for results in power to get commitment and affection from others, and the need to be respected in one's community results in legitimacy power.

Due to patriarchy, men have access to more sources of power than women, such as being able to use force and having more control of resources. Comparatively, women as a group have less interchangeable types of power than men: obligation and sexual access. In other words, women's power comes from the feelings of obligation and control they create in their intimate and familial relationships. Men have more types of power at their disposal that are less dependent on others.[17]

Why does this matter when we are talking about parental alienation? We believe that the answer to this question can help to explain why many special interest groups are resistant to changes in laws pertaining to parental alienation and equal parenting custody orders. Feeling loved and cared for is a basic human need, and this is one of the few domains where women derive power. Women are often labeled as being more empathetic and "better" at relationships than men, and many believe they are inherently more nurturing and better caregivers as well.[18,19] Women possess power when they can create feelings of obligation and commitment among those close to them.[17]

When women started working outside the home, particularly in careers that were not consistent with female stereotypes (such as engineering or business), they have faced backlash from patriarchal and cultural institutions for trying to take on more traditionally masculine roles.[20] Today, women in the U.S. still earn $0.78 for every dollar that men earn, and face considerable discrimination and bias across a large number of industries (e.g., computer science, trades).[21] When women are assertive at work, they are viewed as aggressive because their behavior is inconsistent with the female gender role. Working mothers are viewed as less effective parents than non-working mothers. As described above, legitimacy power is derived from respect in one's community; while men are more legitimate in the work realm, mothers are viewed to be more legitimate parents than fathers because their legitimacy lies in the domestic realm.

With the rise of egalitarianism, men started rejecting the "absentee father" stereotype and became more involved in the domestic realm (where women's power lies), and this has resulted in backlash against them. Men face stigma for being stay-at-home dads and are perceived by others to be weak and insecure.[22] While the backlash for women in the workplace (where men's power lies) has been well documented for many decades, the backlash men face in family courts is comparatively more recent; a new generation of men have been infringing on the source of women's power.

These cultural changes in the role of mothers and fathers provide a backdrop to why we see so much parental alienation today. However, there have been a number of other legislative and cultural changes that have contributed to the problem and make parental alienation easier for some parents than others. We address this next.

Chapter Nine

What Other Legal and Cultural Systems Enable Parental Alienation?

As we reviewed in the last chapter, patriarchy and gender role changes resulting from egalitarianism have led to significant changes to where men and women have power in society. There are also a number of legislative and judicial practices that have made parental alienation easily achievable and increasingly common. The first is an important legislative development that markedly changed the course of how parental alienation cases were handled by family courts, and reflects how power in the domestic realm is misused.

The Domestic Violence against Women Act

Domestic violence has historically been and remains a very serious issue around the world. It is estimated that 1.3 million women and 835,000 men are physically assaulted by an intimate partner in the United States each year.[1] While these statistics are striking, many feel they are underestimated. Men often feel stigmatized and are discouraged from seeking help when abused by a female partner, and many women fail to seek services out of fear of retaliation. Male perpetrators inflict more physical damage than females due to their physical strength,[2] and this has been cited as a reason that legal protection for women and children is needed more than for men.

It wasn't until relatively recently that domestic violence received public recognition; in 1994 the U.S. Congress passed the Domestic Violence against Women Act, which imposed severe and tough provisions against men for committing domestic violence against women. This act was long overdue and provided considerable funding for much needed domestic violence services such as shelters for victims.[3] The act was reauthorized and signed into law by President Obama in 2013,[4] and it extended services to native women, LGBT populations, college students and youth, and also included sexual assault, dating violence, and stalking. Considerable amounts of additional funding were allocated for victims' services, primarily to meet the needs of women and children.

The act was purposefully given a gendered "frame" to make clear that there are disparities in how many women and men are victimized. Law school instructors often only train students on how to handle domestic violence cases in which women are the victims.[5] Recently, legal scholars and advocacy groups have started to argue that having a violence against "women" act suggests that men are not victims of domestic violence, however a large proportion (39% or more) of victims are. In fact, despite challenges from some researchers, there is considerable evidence summarized across many research studies that women are just as or even more physically aggressive and violent than men, [2,6] particularly when provoked.[7]

Equal treatment under the law has not been applied by law enforcement or social services for domestic violence. [6,8] Many men struggle to find shelters, police protection, and other means of support when they are victims. Indeed, many targeted fathers we interviewed were victims of domestic violence and they faced ridicule, ostracism, and disbelief when they shared their experiences with law enforcement, judicial officers, and even family and friends. Some of the fathers we interviewed described in great detail how their ex-wives would continuously throw things and hit them, and one father had to reach over to forcefully move his ex-wife away from him to get her to stop. Episodes such as this were recalled with great regret, and fathers were offered keen advice from other men to not engage in *any* interaction that could be construed as domestic violence, regardless of the provocation. Most of the fathers we interviewed knew the police would not believe them if they called for help, so they just packed up their belongings and left their homes.

The reason this legislative act is important for our understanding of parental alienation is because of how powerful false allegations can be in an alienator's arsenal. We heard many fathers and a few mothers in our interviews refer to claims of abuse as the "silver bullet" because there was almost nothing that could be provided by the accused in their defense to prove their innocence. Some scholars have tried to argue that false allegations are rare,[9] however research indicates that how such cases are investigated and identified is severely flawed. A recent study found that 86% of alienated parents had received court penalties (e.g., jail time) due to false accusations of abuse.[10]

When a parent provides false testimony about abuse or they coerce a child into reporting false events to a mandatory reporter (e.g., school counselor), the accused parent is subjected to lengthy investigations and oftentimes restriction in their parenting time. The accused parent is guilty until proven innocent. The burden of proof for domestic violence in family courts and social services is low. One father we interviewed was repeatedly investigated by child protective services due to anonymous phone calls reporting abuse. When he asked the caseworkers what proof they had for the allegations, he was told directly that *they did not need evidence, and that a simple claim was enough to subject him to an investigation.* Even when such accusations are rendered false, there are little to no legal ramifications for the false accuser. Without deterrents, such behaviors continue.

Many of our interviewees described stories of the alienating parent filing for and obtaining a restraining/protection order due to stated fears of domestic violence. For example, one father drove to pick up his son from his ex-wife's home. He got out of his car and stayed in the street while his ex-wife came outside and started yelling at him. She then proceeded to throw sticks and rocks at him, telling him to leave her property even though it was his day to visit with his son. He got back in his car and drove away. The next day he was served with papers ordering a protection order such that he could not come within 50 ft. of his ex-wife. In many states of the U.S., a woman only needs to say she feels threatened to get a protection order. No evidence is needed.

We are well aware that fears of violence are real and well founded in the lives of many women around the world, and that women are at special risk for encountering domestic violence during the divorce process. However, when domestic violence and child abuse or neglect are claimed, particularly when there appears to be high conflict between parents and/or presence of a possible personality disorder, *these accusations need to be thoroughly investigated* by police and other legal and mental health professionals on a case-by-case basis. Evidence should be evaluated critically, and one person's "word" should not be the only evidence considered. Simply accepting someone's word provides license to a parent who would like to manipulate the legal system. Many parents make false accusations in order to distance their children from the other parent simply because they can, and this behavior is much more common than many would like to believe.

Unlike other crimes, law enforcement and judicial systems have front-ended responses (e.g., always arrest) to cases of domestic violence due to beliefs that these crimes are qualitatively different than other crimes. In many ways they are, because violent partners do often retaliate if a victim calls the police--if an arrest is not made when there is actual violence occurring, the victim is at even greater risk after calling the police than before. The front-ended response, therefore, is a precautionary measure just in case the perpetrator will retaliate. Unfortunately, the accused person's case is not processed in the court system the way other crimes are. Persuasive evidence of guilt is admitted oftentimes without scrutiny and would not be considered admissible in any other criminal case. As a result, there are many biases in how domestic violence cases are adjudicated and therefore there are many false convictions.[11]

Although the Domestic Violence against Women Act is well intended and can protect many people who are legitimate victims, our opinion based on considerable research evidence is that it is being misused in its current form to alienate children from a parent, and this is creating substantial problems for our family courts and criminal justice systems. *False claims of abuse undermine the protection that this act provides for* real *victims of domestic violence; we need to stop encouraging its misuse.* Abuse claims need to be investigated and real evidence must be provided. When the claim is found to be false, then the accuser should be punished.

The battle between feminist and child advocates and father's rights groups

Over the last few years, there has been considerable conflict between feminists, child advocates, and father's rights groups on the topic of parental alienation. Many advocates for abused women and children are resistant to changes in laws related to shared parenting arrangements or addressing parental alienation, and they argue that judicial officers, child custody evaluators, and other court-ordered facilitators overlook or dismiss issues related to child abuse, neglect, and domestic violence in their decisions.[12,13] Unfortunately, this belief is not grounded in evidence that we have reviewed so far;[12] claims of abuse and neglect are given *considerable* weight and prosecuted with little to no evidence, particularly when accusations are made about the father because of stereotypes about men being more aggressive and violent than mothers.

Some researchers have argued that the resistance of feminist and child advocate groups to the parental alienation term lies primarily in a) a belief that children *never* lie about abuse, b) a denial that parents can influence or brainwash a child to believe false allegations, and c) a dismissal of claims that children align with one parent over another. Many of these groups essentially believe that *all* parental alienation is justified (because fathers are abusive), and therefore alienation is just one form of estrangement.[13] Some advocates have gone so far as to propose that accusing a parent of parental alienation in court should be a criminal offence and punishable by law,[14] which would remove any legal recourse for the targeted parent of alienation.

Despite claims made by such feminists and child advocates, false allegations of abuse *do* occur frequently in divorce and custody disputes, but exactly how frequently remains uncertain.[15] Prevalence could be easily tested if resources are devoted to investigating it because there are many ways to determine whether allegations are false. True allegations of domestic violence are more often denied than false ones[16, 17] and children who are actually abused often experience considerable ambivalence toward the abusive parent. These children also offer contradictory testimony when they try to recall exact events that support their abuse claims. When the allegations are false, such children appear to have no guilt or ambivalence towards the "offending" parent. Even when the targeted parent, or others, provide real evidence to contradict the belief that abuse has occurred, alienated children refuse to abandon their perceptions.

There has been recent controversy about an experiment conducted by Miguel Clemente and Dolores Padilla-Racero,[18] who attempted to test the idea that children can be coerced into lying about a verbally aggressive event. Half the children in their sample observed a verbally aggressive event and the other half did not. Then, in another phase of the study, these children were asked to report on what they had observed. The researchers also manipulated whether the children were led to believe that the aggressor would be a future teacher of theirs to make the experiment resemble a "high pressure" situation. The authors concluded from their data that children cannot be coerced to lie, and that the parental alienation concept should not be used in the legal system at all.

We believe this study's conclusions are erroneously drawn from faulty methods. The researchers treated the influence (pressure) of the experimenters and their assistants on the children as equivalent to how parents are able to influence their own offspring. This assumption is not supported by *any* theoretical or research evidence. Children are highly dependent on their parents for their physical and emotional needs, and this puts them in a less powerful position in the family system. Powerful individuals, such as parents have *considerable* social influence on those dependent on them.[19] The children in the study did not have long, established and loving attachment bonds to the experimenters; the experimenters had less power and ability to influence or coerce the children to lie than a parent would.

Alienating parents can (and often do) withhold love, affection, and other rewards when a child doesn't do what pleases them, and may even punish a child for not reporting to others their own warped or fabricated version of the truth. While experimental research on parental alienation is desperately needed (see Chapter 3), this particular study was not objective and was poorly executed—the conclusions made it clear that there was an agenda to deny the existence of parental alienation. Other critics have requested that this particular study should be withdrawn from publication altogether due to the poor methodology employed.[20]

Allegations of abuse can be addressed with more stringent evidentiary requirements and investigative procedures, and parental behaviors involving the coercion of a child to make false allegations can be observed and factually verified.[13] Unfortunately, resistance to changing how custody and parental alienation cases are handled still remains among some feminist and child advocate groups. We believe that this resistance is largely due to the power that the custodial parent (typically the mother) provides.

In response to the resistance that some feminist and child advocate groups have posed to legal and social reforms related to equal parenting time initiatives and other family law reforms, many father's rights groups have been very critical of them. We have seen frequent posts made by men on some father's rights Facebook discussion groups denying that there is a gender pay gap, claiming that colleges and universities are bastions of feminist radicals who persecute and limit educational access to men, and that there is no such thing as a rape culture in the U.S. We will not spend time disputing each claim made by some of the members of these groups, as doing so detracts from the purpose of this book. However, it is important to note here that the claims they are making reflect how defensive these groups are about the power they have in patriarchal society. They feel threatened by women who they perceive as wanting to "take" power from them in domains where they have it (e.g., work, higher education). The mothers arguing against the existence of parental alienation are threatened by fathers because they are perceived as trying to take power in an area that is "theirs," the domestic realm.

Michael Flood has noted that while many separated fathers turn to these father's rights groups for support, a number of members are more concerned with re-establishing their parental authority than having greater involvement with their children; therefore many men do not often get the support they need.[21] While we agree that such groups are limited in the types of support they can offer to targeted parents, it is important to note that some parents join such groups in order to do something constructive with their grief and to get information about how to have a relationship with their children again. Many of these fathers do not agree with the "bashing" of women and feminists that commonly happens on these social media pages. One father we interviewed described engaging in many arguments with other men on these discussion group forums, but he still remained a member of the groups because he *did* agree with them on the need to have equality in parental rights.

We believe that the extreme, polarized positions of both sides of this argument are very negative and counterproductive. Both want equal rights...in the domain where they currently possess less power. Both are territorial and emotionally protective about areas where they currently possess more power than the other. They want something from the other side, but do not see that they are being hypocritical about not promoting equality where they have more power. Individuals occupying the opposite sides of this battle are very rational about what they believe to be a serious societal offense against them, and yet they are irrational in their denial of evidence that undermines their positions. The result is a lack of empathy and understanding of the other side's perspective.

This stalemate provides support to our position that this battle is about power. Parental alienation has been treated as a personal issue, but it instead reflects a larger cultural battle over power in the domestic realm. Both of us strongly identify as feminists because we subscribe to the belief that *all people should be treated fairly and be afforded the same rights.* We disagree with any individual or group, whether they are feminists, child advocates, or father's rights groups, who want equality in one domain, but do not recognize or work towards addressing inequality where they have advantage.

Rise in narcissism

Aside from the Domestic Violence against Women Act and other social changes regarding gender roles, there have also been a number of social changes that we believe are also influencing parental alienating behaviors. Between 1976 and 2006, Jean Twenge and colleagues found that average narcissism scores of U.S. college students rose 30%.[22] This problem is not unique to the U.S., either. Some blame the use of social media as being a culprit for this rise, and others blame the individualistic culture of the U.S. and constant overpraising of children for everything, such as giving a medal or trophy for simply showing up. In a prior chapter, we discussed how narcissism was one of the personality disorders associated with parental alienating behaviors. Men have higher rates of narcissism than women, but women are catching up fast.

We believe that the prevalence of parental alienation may be partially associated with these increasing levels of narcissism. There are many individuals with extreme narcissistic traits who are very dangerous towards others, but are not severe enough to be considered a full-blown personality disorder. The cognitive and emotionally driven behaviors associated with narcissism have serious and at times dangerous ramifications for interpersonal relations and parenting. Narcissists are self-centered and have an inability to feel empathy, both for the plight of the other parent as well as for the children who suffer the loss of them. This self-centeredness makes parenting and post-separation cooperation and negotiation with them nearly impossible.

Additionally, the importance of this rise in narcissism may impact how children react to parental alienation. When an alienating parent idealizes a child and lets them do whatever they want in their home, these children grow to expect this treatment from others. Shame is the emotion that fuels much of what narcissists do--- when they feel shame about themselves, they lash out at those around them to make them feel as bad as they do. They point to others' weaknesses so as to avoid their own.[23] Both parents are important to a child's identity, and when an alienator disparages one parent, the child ultimately feels shame and dislike for part of themselves. This may lead to greater levels of narcissism in the child as a way to cope with this problem. We hope that more research will be conducted that directly examines the relationship between parental alienation and the development of narcissism in children.

In addition, narcissism is fueled when a child is given the opportunity to choose between one parent and another. *Does a child really have the ability or maturity to choose wisely? Why does society allow children the "open space" to make a choice between parents, rather than provide supports so that* both *parents can remain in the child's life?* The degree of impact these rising rates of narcissism and their impact on children needs to be explored; this is a very important avenue for research on parental alienation.

Female-to-female aggression

Parental alienation largely involves an alienator's aggression against the targeted parent, however we saw time and again that alienation increased once a new romantic partner entered the picture, primarily when there were mothers and step-mothers (and sometimes even ex-mothers-in-law). As we mentioned earlier, we had only 1 out of 28 step-parents in our survey study identify as a step-father. Why are we seeing so much female-to-female aggression? Until relatively recently, it was politically incorrect to study female aggression. Researchers could rarely get funding to study it because many battered women's advocates pushed and lobbied to draw attention to (and focus almost exclusively) on male violence.[24] This cultural bias has led to a very skewed and distorted understanding of what we know about human aggression.

We do know that women and men exhibit aggressive behaviors differently. For example, women use more indirect and relational forms of aggression than men (who tend to be more verbal and direct); women prefer to use others to hurt their targets.[25] This gender difference is consistent with what many parents described to us in their interviews. Many mothers used teachers, neighbors, friends, and family to accomplish their alienating goals, and we did not hear targeted mothers share as many examples of this when the fathers were the alienators (unless a step-mother was involved).

Regardless of what types of aggressive strategies are used, the question remains as to *why* we heard so many examples of female-to-female aggression in our study. Since the early to mid-2000s, researchers have predominantly used an evolutionary approach to understand why women aggress against each other. A primary motivator of behavior is reproductive success; not just having children, but raising them to reproductive age. For the most part, the only studies (so far) using an evolutionary framework to understand female-to-female human aggression have explained it as a way to compete for or retain mates. For example, Steven Arnocky and colleagues have found that women who compared themselves more to other women's appearance use more indirect aggressive behaviors (e.g., gossiping, derogating their character) towards them, particularly when they experienced jealousy.[26]

These mate guarding behaviors are adaptive at fending off potential rivals-- the mother/step-mother may believe that if she makes the step-mother/mother look like a horrible person (e.g., a slut, a "homewrecker," a monster), she has a chance to win the father back or earn more favor if she is the step-mother. Many alienators have a hard time moving on from the relationship or letting go of the father, so this is one plausible explanation. Obviously, degrading the other woman in front of the children also wins their favor, but the theoretical explanation that has been tested so far has largely focused only on motives associated with securing and retaining a mate.

We have considered an alternate explanation related to motives that ensure children reach reproductive age. Among other animal species, research has long documented mothers' protective behaviors of their young-- if there is a perceived threat of injury or death, for example, animals will engage in protective behaviors (e.g., blocking access).[27] This protectiveness often is in response to other males who are not the father (such as in the case of stallions and lions who would kill offspring that are not theirs), and this may explain why fathers may alienate if the mother remarries. In a review of non-human primate female social relationships, Elisabeth Sterk and colleagues have proposed that changes in habitats can affect how females interact with each other. For example, female red howler monkeys in Venezuela (individuals and as multiples) often target and evict other females as a way to regulate the number of females in the group. In their review, however, they note that there has not been any real agreement or unifying theory about why different patterns of female-to-female aggression occurs; there is too great a variability across primates to draw that conclusion.[28]

We have asked numerous experts of human aggression about what they think is happening in cases where mothers are aggressing against step-mothers and girlfriends, and vice versa. Many agreed with our hypothesis that the real threat of losing one's offspring to the father or another women may motivate the mother to alienate. Similarly, the step-mother may want to secure her position with her new mate, and can accomplish this more effectively if she "replaces" the other mother— alienation is a tool that can make both things happen.

We have noted several times that we did not see as much father/step-father parental alienation. In many species, males do not want to raise another male's offspring; in fact many will kill offspring produced by another male (e.g., lions). Father/step-father alienation may exist, particularly when one of the parents has a personality disorder, but more research needs to be conducted to fully understand why we see different patterns of aggressive behavior among different parental relationships, as this is important for our understanding of parental alienation.

A great many legislative acts and cultural changes have contributed to what appears to be a rise in parental alienation. Power associated with the mother and father role has also resulted in intense resistance to clinical, legal, and judicial interventions designed to address this problem. We will next explore how the parental expectations we have (which are impacted by all of these factors), are contributing to the problem.

CHAPTER TEN

HOW DO PERCEPTIONS OF PARENTING ABILITY AFFECT HOW ALIENATORS ACCOMPLISH THEIR GOALS?

Our beliefs about what makes someone a "good" parent are directly influenced by our social and cultural contexts. In Chapter 8, we discussed how patriarchy impacts our expectations of mothers and fathers. Essentially, patriarchy acts as a lens and filters what our perceptions of what a "good" parent means. This lens helps explain why mothers can generally alienate much more easily than fathers, and under what circumstances fathers are able to be the alienator themselves. Stereotypes influence our perceptions and judgments of parents who do not meet our expectations for being a mother or father. Even in very egalitarian cultures (e.g., Norway and Sweden), traditional parental role expectations still linger because such norms take long periods of time to change.[1]

Fathers as the target of alienation

Today there are still strong stereotypes that men are not as nurturing or empathetic as women, which are traits valued in the raising of healthy children. These stereotypes result in biases in how fathers' parenting abilities are judged compared to mothers. Mothers act as "maternal gatekeepers" even in intact relationships, such that they express behaviors and attitudes about the father that encourage or discourage the father from being involved with raising a child. The mothers most likely to "close the gate" tend to be perfectionistic and critical of the father, and limit their involvement early on because they have the power in the domestic arena to do this.[2]

In a study of divorced mothers, many believed that men were not as good at parenting as them, and could not be trusted with running a household. These mothers also believed that fathers could not be emotionally nurturing with their children, and they expressed concerns about their ability to be patient, particularly with small children. Importantly, the researcher conducting the study recommended that practitioners be aware of their own biases in underestimating a father's parenting abilities during custody evaluations, especially when a mother covertly or overtly implies that he is deficient.[3]

Particularly insidious is how courts and many mental health professionals perceive the attachment between fathers and children. Due to restrictions in visitation time that fathers often endure prior to custody evaluations (e.g., work, interference with parenting time by the mother), interactions between fathers and children can appear disconnected when they are able to spend time together in front of an evaluator or mental health professional. For example, when we see a videotape or observe a father and child who have not seen each other regularly, the interactional style can look like that between a new babysitter and child. Even though the father may use every parenting skill available to him, it is not possible to simulate familiarity and a relaxed atmosphere with one's child when there is a deficit in the amount of time spent with them. Sadly, when children appear insecurely attached with fathers during these observations, it reinforces strong stereotypes of the absentee, or detached father that is hard to ignore. While the old adage of "it is not quantity, but quality that counts" is sometimes true, in the case of parenting time, it is both quality *and* quantity that matter.

Many judges make decisions about custody based on stereotypes. In one study, 79% of fathers reported that the judge in their case used very inappropriate and biased language to describe them, explicitly saying that fathers were less important and were deadbeats.[4] In their defense, some fathers have organized national fatherhood initiatives (http://www.fatherhood.org/) that offer trainings with "father engagement certificates" which can be earned to help fathers in custody disputes where the mothers have tried to portray them as being incapable or absent parents. These initiatives are designed to empower men to obtain equal rights in a domain where women have advantage, much like trainings and seminars are offered to women on negotiation and leadership skills to be competitive in the career world. Therefore, patriarchy puts fathers at a disadvantage to mothers in the domestic realm due to how it impacts perceptions of their parenting ability.

Mothers as the target of alienation

Mothers are certainly targets of parental alienation as well. While there were a few severe cases, the majority of mothers that we interviewed reported less severe alienation than the fathers we talked to, and most mothers still had *some* contact or regular visitation with their children. One reason for this difference is due to the modern patriarchal lens that ties "mom" more closely to being female than "father" is to being male; in other words it is more difficult to separate a woman from the positively valued parenting role than it is for a man.[5] Because of this disparity, alienating mothers from their children can be more difficult (although not impossible) for fathers than the other way around. In order to effectively alienate a mother, the father (and others assisting him) must get others to perceive her as unmotherly, such as portraying her as someone who cares more about her career than her children, as someone who is abusive or neglectful, or as someone who is mentally ill.

Working mothers have faced challenges in the courts when they have violated gender norms that can be used against them in custody battles. For example, working mothers are rated as being less effective parents than non-working mothers.[6] We interviewed many successful and highly educated mothers who were either the breadwinners of the family or had the same income or status job as their ex-husbands prior to separation and divorce. Each of these mothers was accused of caring more about her career than her children, and as being a cold and distant mother because she was filling a work role that was not traditional for women (e.g., physician). Essentially, she was punished for fulfilling the male gender breadwinner role.

Due to expectations of being more responsible for parenting than fathers, mothers are also often blamed more when things go wrong with children. For example, a mother is perceived to be more responsible for, negligent, and less competent if an infant dies than a father is. Men are also more likely to recommend more severe and longer punishments for mothers than fathers if they view mothers as incompetent.[7] Therefore, when mothers can be faulted for problems with the raising of children, they are perceived to be worse parents and are more likely to be punished by the courts than fathers.

If a father can get traction in court or with mental health professionals to use exaggerated or false claims of abuse or neglect with a mother, it is likely harder for women to erase or minimize this from their records than fathers, who generally are always expected to be abusive or neglectful. The parent who goes against expectations is generally punished, unless the behavior is in the positive direction. For many mothers, the alienating father promoted an image of himself as being "exemplary." These fathers were able to get considerable leverage to accomplish their alienation when they could prove simultaneously that they were a "great" dad and that the mother fell short of her maternal expectations.

Many mothers we interviewed described how their ex-partner was able to alienate them because they convinced everyone that the she was "crazy." Indeed, one father we interviewed said that his lawyer told him that his only protection in court against this ex's false claims of abuse was to show that the mother was mentally ill. Due to power and status differentials between men and women, women are stereotypically perceived to be more illogical and emotional than men. They are also more easily labeled with mental illness than men, whether they have been legitimately diagnosed or not. Many psychologists have noted a gender bias in the diagnosis of numerous psychological disorders such as depression. Mothers who have been suspected of, or diagnosed with a mental illness, have concerns about maintaining custody of their children.[8] There is evidence in courts that attorneys are gender biased in blaming criminal behaviors on mental illness more for females than males,[9] and that even forensic evaluators, whose opinions weigh heavily in criminal cases, show this same bias.[10] Whether women actually struggle with a mental illness, or are believed to have one, this can be used against them. Ridding oneself of the stigma associated with a mental illness label is not easy.[11]

In short, modern patriarchal culture has impacted where mothers and fathers obtain power, how they wield it, and can explain why each is perceived differently as parents. It also can help explain why certain strategies work for men and women to alienate the other parent. Mothers who want to alienate are able to do so because a large number of factors provide her advantage: the parenting/domestic role is currently her place of legitimacy, she has the Violence against Women Act to wield more effectively than men, and she has strong cultural biases that favor her as a parent over the father. Fathers who want to alienate can be successful if there is some way they can manipulate the system so that the mother is seen as somehow "unmotherly" due to her career, mental illness, physical abuse, or neglect. The burden of proof for the father is higher, but with the right evidence (whether legitimate or false) and willing assistants (e.g., step-mothers, brainwashed children, teachers, neighbors), he can be successful. Our hope is that in explaining why these techniques are effective, the information will not be used for ill: rather, if we understand *why* they are effective, then mothers and fathers can better protect themselves and more effective interventions can be developed.

CHAPTER ELEVEN

HOW CAN PARENTAL ALIENATION BE

RECOGNIZED AND HANDLED MORE

EFFECTIVELY?

Parental alienation is not a new problem for mental health professionals and family courts. There have been a number of attempts to address this problem, each with varying degrees of success. Despite these interventions, prevalence of alienation is still high. We believe that the problem is persisting largely due to not fully understanding parental alienation from a systemic perspective, as well as due to the legal system and society ignoring its pervasiveness—essentially sweeping it under the rug. We briefly review here how professionals and the legal and judicial professions have handled parental alienation so far, and importantly, we suggest alternative and enhanced solutions.

Assessment of the child

We believe that parental alienation is a problem that many children of intact *and* divorced families face, but it is rarely clinically assessed. Alienated children are accustomed to hiding their real emotions and presenting a "false self" that may not be in their best interest; they will appear more mature, or severely regressed than their actual age. Mental health professionals should be trained in and understand parental alienation and should assess *all* children who are involved in divorce or who present with symptoms of trauma. This assessment should include a long, detailed, and very critical investigation of the history of the family, as well as interviews with collateral contacts provided by *both* parents, particularly if there are claims of abuse. *When one or more children are enmeshed with a parent, the enmeshed parent is often the parental alienator.* Observations and interviews with both parents should be standard practice, and special attention should be paid to how children act in both homes. Any disparaging remarks made by either parent about each other to a child and other signs of alienation tactics being practiced should raise a red flag.

Interviews and observations with the children should also be conducted to determine whether responses are scripted, and whether beliefs and memories about past events are highly discrepant from one or another of the parents. In addition, a standardized battery of clinical assessments should be conducted to understand each child's level of functioning. Psychological symptoms resembling attention deficits, anxiety, and conduct disorders among children should also be considered possible symptoms of trauma and stress resulting from parental conflict and alienation, rather than as something that is a problem residing in the child. *These issues should be treated in systemic ways rather than just using medication to "fix" the child's problems.* When a child has been told many negative things about a parent (and there is little or no substantiation for it), this should be treated as a cause of trauma—the child's attachment to the parent is damaged and disrupted with such actions, and real or perceived abandonment is a very painful experience for a child.

Assessment of the parent

Trying to identify whether someone is a parental alienator has been a difficult task. Some investigators have attempted to use clinical tools such as the Minnesota Multiphasic Personality Inventory-2 and have found that alienating parents tend to respond to certain subscales in a defensive manner and to try and appear "flawless."[1] Ana Lavadera and colleagues have created a tool to identify severe forms of parental alienation based on Gardner's (2004) criteria. While this tool has not been validated and has only been applied to a small number (12 families) of court cases, such a move is promising in terms of helping to develop criteria for legal professionals to use in identifying such families.[2] Obviously, using an assessment tool such as this will first entail getting mental health and legal professionals to accept alienation as a real phenomenon and to stop denying its existence.

Although not all parents with narcissism, borderline, and antisocial personality disorders will alienate their children, there is enough evidence to suggest that such parents are more likely to do so, whether conscious or not. At times when custody and parenting plan recommendations or changes are being made, we strongly believe that *all* parents and other adults involved with direct care of the children (e.g., step-parents) be thoroughly assessed for personality disorders using valid instruments. When there is an indication or presence of a personality disorder (or features of these disorders not meeting the full diagnostic criteria of the DSM-5), then claims of abuse, ability to cooperate, and other important parenting qualities of this individual should be viewed with a more critical eye, free of personal biases. Depending upon the severity of their disorder, courts should also consider requiring therapy for the parent.

Throughout this book, we have discussed how observations of parent-child interactions between the targeted parent and their child(ren) may appear strained, unattached, or difficult because of parental alienation. It is important to consider the reasons that the relationship appears this way, and that it may not be an indication of the parent's abilities or their love for their children. Many targeted parents have had little time with their children, and they must spend all their short periods of time together getting to know each other again. If anything, we believe that signs of distance between the parent and the child should be an indication that further investigation is needed, particularly for the overly connected, enmeshed parent. Evaluators should be particularly critical of this parent's claims of domestic violence and/or abuse when there is no factual evidence to support them, or when actions are exaggerated to make it appear there is more threat and danger than there actually exists. There should be a suspension of judgment until the evidence can be heard and evaluated, just like any other criminal act.

Psychotherapeutic interventions

Parental alienation is difficult to address in psychotherapy. Oftentimes, the alienating parent either resists therapy for their children out of fear of exposure, or pulls the children out of the therapeutic relationship when they feel it is undermining their alienating goals.[3] For example, a therapist may challenge a child's false belief in abuse occurring with the targeted parent, and if the child starts to question the validity of this "truth," the alienator ends therapy or finds another therapist.

Therapists have recommended that the alienator's needs should be addressed in order to stop parental alienation. Because alienators often lack the ability to negotiate boundaries and they project their needs onto their children, they need education and outside intervention in order to address their behavior.[4] Family therapy with professionals who are well-trained in parental alienation dynamics and parent education would be useful here. Many alienated children derive some satisfaction from their enmeshed role with the alienator because being a confidante makes them feel powerful. Alienating the other parent also helps them to subconsciously cope with conflicting feelings, so addressing these issues in psychotherapy can be difficult with these children.

Psychotherapeutic interventions are also useful in helping children see how the roles the alienator has put them in are not healthy. Paz Toran and colleagues attempted to do such a thing in short-term (16 weeks, 90 minutes each session) group therapy with a group of children aged 6-16 years old who had refused to see one of their parents for more than four months.[5] The children met with therapists in groups, and the parents met separately with a mix of alienated and non-alienated parents. Using a therapeutic approach that involved

coping and interpersonal skills training, the goal of these
groups was to address intense emotions and to try and
change visitation patterns between the parents and
children. Among the children, anxiety and depression
decreased up to three years later compared to a control
group of children who did not attend the groups. The
parents also reported greater levels of parental
cooperation after participating, and those children whose
parents were the most psychologically disturbed
benefitted most from the treatment; they essentially
learned new coping skills that their parent was unable to
teach them.[5]

School-based interventions

Schools offer an excellent intervention point to
address parental alienation because children are away
from their dysfunctional family environment for many
hours each day. Court ordered parenting plans often
incorporate schools into them, such as having parenting
time start at the release of school on certain days, and
ordering parents to have specific types of educational
rights. Unfortunately, many school systems are ill-
equipped to deal with the destruction and chaos that
alienators bring when they try to enlist school personnel
into their campaign against the targeted parent. Trainings
designed to assist teachers in identifying alienating tactics

and how they impact their students are a starting point. Developing school-wide policies on how to handle parental conflicts when school personnel are involved are also necessary.

Guidance counselors and school psychologists can also play an important role in helping children to cope with parental alienation. One school-based intervention was developed by Amy Baker, and the aim of the program was to teach problem-solving skills to all children who are from families that have experienced divorce or separation.[6] The program covers critical thinking skills to help the children understand if they are adopting false ideas, helps them consider options besides obeying or disobeying, teaches them to listen to their heart so that they can get close to their own sense of truth, and offers support. A facilitator leads 20 weekly sessions to a small group of children, where they are presented with vignettes about family situations (e.g., loyalty conflicts) and children are asked to use problem-solving skills to resolve the conflict. The program is fully manualized, but thus far it has not been evaluated.

Our hope is that more school-based interventions are developed and evaluated due to the promise they hold to teach children effective coping skills to handle the conflicts they are experiencing in their family. Schools can play an important role in mediating between parents in a way that buffers the impact parental alienation has on everyone involved. We are currently exploring such solutions in our own work and hope to test their effectiveness soon.

Judicial interventions

Without clear judicial responses to violations of parenting plans and other alienating behaviors, parental alienation escalates over time.[7] An estimated 80% of parents who refuse to comply with court orders about contact or visitation with the other parent are mothers, and they use any excuse possible to limit contact, such as claiming that children do not want to see their father or that their own schedules will not make visitation possible (e.g., school, work). Over a 24-month period, alienating parents are likely to seek court intervention to get sole custody of their children at least twice, claiming that their children are anxious or have nightmares about being with the other parent, or that the child has delusions about the other parent persecuting or abusing them.[8]

Judicial involvement is often the targeted parent's last resort to address the alienation and see their children, but taking action can serve as a catalyst for even more alienation.[9] The custodial parent has an unfair advantage in this situation because they can manipulate the children and situation for their benefit; many tell the children that the targeted parent is "out to get them." This further aligns the children with the alienator.

Alienated parents do not often seek court intervention due to financial concerns or fears of putting their children in the "middle." One father we spoke with backed down at a court hearing when he heard that his ex-wife was going to have his children testify on the stand against him. He could not believe his ex-wife would ever put the children in that situation, and he could not bear to let her follow through with it for his children's sake. Even more parents are counseled out of pursuing legal intervention at all, being told by their lawyers that they will never win. While courts often have sympathy for the non-custodial parent, they still rule in favor of the children's desires, which are severely warped by the custodial parent.[10]

When cases do finally appear in family court, magistrates and judges often have a hard time distinguishing between estrangement and alienation, so making a clear determination that is in the best interest of the child poses problems. In many cases, Parental Alienation Syndrome (PAS) is not considered an admissible argument in court, despite there being hundreds of peer-reviewed papers and many clinical books documenting its existence. In order to find an expert's testimony admissible in court, there are two standards that are commonly used, the Frye and Daubert standards. When the Frye standard (*Frye v. United States*, 293 F. 1013; D.C. Cir. 1923) is applied, the court must determine whether the way evidence was obtained is generally accepted by experts in the field, which in this case would be clinical and developmental psychologists working with children and families. Given the controversial history and resistance to the use of PAS in courts by feminists and child advocates, and the belief that PAS is based on "junk science" (discussed in Chapter 3), this standard has made acceptance of expert testimony in court about parental alienation very difficult for targeted parents.

The Frye standard has been replaced in many courts with the Daubert standard (*Daubert v. Merrell Dow Pharmaceuticals, Inc.*, 509 U.S. 579, 1993), which allows the trial judge to use several factors to determine whether scientific testimony is admissible, include whether the methods used to make a determination are scientifically valid and tested, whether it has been subjected to peer-review and publication, whether there is an identifiable error rate, whether there are standards in its application and operation, and whether there is widespread acceptance in the scientific community for its existence. The Daubert standard has replaced the Frye standard in Federal courts, and many states have adopted this approach, but some have not. These standards have important ramifications for whether parents can introduce parental alienation as a defense or enter a motion for enforcement or change to their parenting plans.

One important consideration that judges and magistrates should consider is the type of relationship the targeted parent had with their child(ren) in the past. If the relationship was warm and loving, and then over time the child has rejected and been coaxed into believing horrible things about them, then the reasons for this change in attitude need to be fully understood. It is also very difficult for alienated parents to prove alienation because a child's rejection of them can be interpreted by professionals and courts as being due to estrangement (and justified) depending on how much influence the alienating parent has had on them. Their apparent rejection can also depend on the age and level of enmeshment of the child with the alienator and how much time has elapsed since separation. Proving alienation can be very expensive as well, because independent experts and private mental health professionals must be hired to provide their professional opinions on the case. Most parents lack the financial resources to do this.

Parental alienation cases that finally do make it to court are often very long and complicated. If a judge determines that parental alienation is occurring, they are then faced with the difficult decision of how to remedy the problem. Some cases have been perpetuated for so many years that a court order to repair the relationship between the targeted parent and the child(ren) can cause more harm than good. In some cases where alienation has been demonstrated, judges grant joint custody to both parents to "send a message" to the alienator that both parents are important in a child's life, with the intent to minimize instability for the child.[7] Sometimes the non-custodial parent alienates the child during their visits, and supervision needs to be ordered for their visits to ensure that the child is not distressed by anything the alienating parent says or does.

If an alienating parent denies or restricts access of the child without court approval, the targeted parent must usually file a motion of contempt with the court. Hearings to determine contempt of court can take months to be heard, resulting in a targeted parent not seeing their child(ren) for significant lengths of time. The result?

Their relationship with their children becomes even more disconnected and distant. Sanctions for violations of court orders, such as fines or jail time, are recommended to stop alienation, but they are not often applied or enforced.[10]

The parents we interviewed reported great variability in how the courts responded to violations of court orders, particularly restrictions in parenting time and visitation. Recently, a Michigan judge in the U.S. sent three children to juvenile detention for refusing to have lunch with their alienated father, only to later reverse her judgement and order them to attend a therapeutic summer camp to try and repair their relationship.[11] If one parent has primary physical custody and the other has alternating weekends, there needs to be consequences for the custodial parent for not abiding by this contract, not punishment of the children. The legal system fails many targeted parents by not enforcing parenting-time arrangements,[12] and this exacerbates the problem. The alienator learns that they can do what they want without fear of consequence.

There are also financial incentives for parents to alienate. In the U.S. and many other countries (e.g., Australia), child support is calculated based upon the income of the parents and the amount of custody they have. As a result, the parent who has more custodial time with the children is entitled to more child support. Many alienating parents maintain and even improve their quality of life after violating court orders for this reason.[9] Some countries (e.g., Sweden) use a formula to calculate child support that is based on the cost to raise a child rather than income. This type of policy is preferable, as it takes away the financial incentive to have a monopoly on custody.

Likewise, if equal parenting time is the default, then both parents are equally responsible for the day-to-day raising of the child; child support would no longer be necessary. We interviewed numerous parents who said that the alienating parent was able to get more child support for the time they "stole" from them by restricting their parenting time (against court orders). In other words, the targeted parents had to pay child support for the parenting time the alienating parent withheld from them (and had been ordered to them by the court). One father we interviewed called this "taxation without representation."

Many parents we interviewed told us that listening to their attorneys was one of the biggest mistakes they made. Some attorneys coached the alienator on how to argue that abuse or violence happened in order to get custody of their children, and this was when the alienating process began. Many attorneys also recommended that parents just "settle" and admit to allegations of abuse when there was no evidence and the parent was falsely accused. We recommend that there be mandated training for family law attorneys on parental alienation, and this includes learning strategies for countering parental alienation tactics. For example, one father we interviewed had his divorce delayed for years due to his ex-wife's attorney claiming "acts of God" happening to her (e.g., her house being struck by lightning) that prevented important hearings from happening. These legal delays resulted in months of not being able to see his children and gave the alienator unlimited time to indoctrinate them with lies about him.[12]

Judges and magistrates change frequently across court systems. When a new judge or magistrate is appointed, they do not have a sufficient chance to see the whole range or history of parental alienating behaviors of the offending parent.[12] Many families embroiled in court battles due to parental alienation are in court for decades of their lives, so this turnover has serious consequences for how alienation is handled, if at all. One father we spoke to said he had 8 different judges deciding on his case over a 20-year period. One judge, who was on the bench for 5 years, started noticing patterns in his ex-wife's alienating behaviors and legal tactics. This judge started sanctioning the mother and the alienation stopped, temporarily. Once a new judge was appointed, the alienation began again. Similarly, social workers and caseworkers investigating claims of abuse (e.g., Child Protection Services) have high turnover. These agencies oftentimes only respond to individual reports and they do not see the entire case history to put each report into context.

Due to frequent turnovers in the staffing of people who have much control over how parenting time and plans are changed and enforced, better systems need to be established for making sure that important historical information about parental behaviors are not lost. Manipulative parents are very good at reframing past events and casting them in a light that makes them look like they are the better parent. When specific details about their alienating tactics are omitted, hidden, or forgotten, then judges, magistrates, guardians ad litem, social workers, and other players are fooled by them. Education about what signs, behaviors, and patterns/strategies alienating parents typically use will also make identification of them easier.

Court systems in other countries have not addressed parental alienation effectively either. Parental alienation is known in Arab-Israeli courts (Shari'a Courts) because under Muslim religious law, parental influence on a child to get them to reject the other parent is considered a sin. Therefore, parental alienation is not viewed lightly; indeed, it is often seen as very harmful to the child. Despite this legal and religious stance on the problem, parental alienation is rarely acknowledged or prosecuted there.[13] In Sweden, parental alienation is considered a family matter. While legal recommendations are made, an alienator is rarely punished, even when they engage in illegal behavior. For example, one mother (who herself was Swedish) reported the targeted father we interviewed (who is American) to Sweden's migration authority, stating that his re-entry into Sweden was illegal and that he should be deported. Given that he had a permanent visa which is given to all parents who have a child living in Sweden, she knowingly and willfully made a false claim to harass him. In addition, she regularly blocked his access to his son, although he moved to Sweden in order to be near him. Despite all of this, she received no legal consequence. Parental alienation is a global problem that is poorly addressed in judicial ways.

Admissible evidence. Many of the parents we interviewed were falsely accused of abusing their children. In order to protect themselves, a great number of parents reported audio and videotaping their interactions with their children on a regular basis. Although it may be their only proof of innocence against false claims of abuse, many courts do not allow parents to admit these recordings as evidence because both parties need to be aware they are being recorded in some jurisdictions. Another motivation these parents had for videotaping was so they could show these interactions to others (such as displays of stalking behaviors by the other parent) and get social validation for what they were experiencing.

Other researchers have found serious problems with family courts in terms of what is allowed as evidence, such as having a heavy reliance on hearsay evidence provided by the lawyers of alienating parents. In one custody hearing, one targeted father we spoke to was not allowed to cross-examine two mental and medical health professionals who were testifying on behalf of his ex-wife because he was told "there was no time" by the magistrate. The testimony provided by these professionals was so blatantly false, he later reported them to their professional licensure boards and both were censured. In other words, the expert witnesses' respective boards took the time to consider the statements of these witnesses under oath, but the family court did not.

We recommend that there be a serious reconsideration of what is considered admissible evidence in family court for claims of abuse and parental alienation, and that due process and codes of conduct be followed for all parties involved with each case. Appeals are often expensive and are rarely overturned, and so there is little oversight to the judicial process. *Court reforms addressing process, admissible evidence, and accountability are necessary.*

Reunification programs that are court involved. In some parental alienation cases, the damage to children is so severe that the child has a pathological and often paranoid bond with the alienating parent. In these cases, the judge can order complete changes in custody and psychotherapy to try and fix the damage the alienator wrought. Unfortunately, court-ordered interventions are often ordered much too late and they are rarely enforced. Some judges intensify alienation by allowing the *alienator* to select the mental health professional that they want to use, and this illustrates a serious lack of understanding or concern for how parental alienation processes operate.[9]

Reparative or reunification therapies are one form of intervention that has been attempted based on the premise that targeted parents need to be unconditionally and emotionally available, as well as have patience and hope that their relationship with their children can get better. The reason for this premise is that despite having false beliefs about past abuse, having conflicts of loyalty, and being very hostile towards a targeted parent, alienated children do want the freedom to have two loving parents. Reunification programs emphasize the importance of children coming to view both parents as valuable in their lives, while at the same time help to create a healthier emotional connection with their alienating parent.

Barbara Jo Fidler and Nicholas Bala have noted that when children are given the opportunity, they can develop an enjoyable relationship with their previously hated parent.[14] Their recommendation is not to view children as having the wisdom to decide about their own long-term social and emotional needs, but to help create a positive connection with both parents. A number of reunification models are available, such as Richard Warshak's *Family Bridges* Program, which is conducted in a retreat setting with one family at a time.[15] A premise of *Family Bridges* is that alienated children need some time away from the favored parent to be able to reconnect with the targeted parent. The program helps children to recreate their identity as loving and needing of both parents. The program also offers a workshop for the alienating parents. At first, the majority of children attending these retreats are reluctant, and many adamantly refuse to go. However, in the end, the retreat offered a way for these children to admit that it is worthwhile to have two caring parents.

Kathleen Reay also has created a retreat program that has reported a 95% success rate called the *Family Reflections Reunification Program, Inc.*[16] This psychoeducational and experiential program requires that families be court-ordered to attend the program which typically runs for 4 days. During this time, the targeted parent and the children work with counselors and are reunified slowly. By the second or third day, the children report starting to feel emotionally safe again with the targeted parent, and there is follow-up care afterwards to continue repairing the relationship. The favored parent seeks counseling with a trained and certified Family Reflections therapist in his or her locale or through a HIPPA-compliant video conferencing service.

Another program called *Overcoming Barriers Family Camp* uses a therapy model in which the intention is to have all parties (children, both parents, step-parents, step-siblings) voluntarily attend and engage in many camp activities.[17] A shared parenting plan is developed while at the camp as well as for after the program ends. Unfortunately, the alienating parent often intrudes on activities when the children are with the targeted parent, such as sending texts or other messages that direct the children on how to feel or how to behave. When the alienator is required by court to not intrude during these visits, the results have been promising. This program is still new and undergoing revisions, although some parents have complained that the alienation only intensified after participation. For example, some children were coerced by the alienating parent to "play along" until the court-ordered camp was finished, and then they severely rejected the targeted parent once again when court involvement ended.

Another intervention was developed by Steven Friedlander and Marjorie Gans Walters called the *Multimodal Family Intervention*.[18] This approach targets different components of the problem, including addressing how the stress of the marital break-up has affected the child, teaching coping strategies to the child, challenging the child's splitting (good/bad or polarized views of the parents), challenging their enmeshment and alignment with the alienator, and restoring co-parenting in the family system. Additionally, Elizabeth Ellis has also recommended that targeted parents should be provided with information about what the children have been told to believe about them, and be encouraged to share contradictory information with the child to decrease the enmeshment between them and the alienating parent.[19] While such an approach may make the targeted parent be seen as less of an enemy, parents must also be careful not to turn the tides too far and make the alienating parent look bad either, even if they *are* acting badly.

When working with the alienator, it is important to underscore the importance of co-parenting, rather than "taking away" or alienating the child from either parent. While custody reversal is sometimes recommended in really severe cases of alienation,[14] such reversal should be viewed only in temporary terms, with the final goal being sharing of parenting responsibility. Thus, *shared parenting is more likely to prevent* severe *alienation than sole custody.* That said, there also needs to be mechanisms in place to prevent milder forms of alienation when there are shared parenting plans--- one or both parents often put their own needs (advertently, or inadvertently) in front of their children when they are aggressing against the other parent. General thinking in this area is that psychotherapy can be useful for mild and moderate cases of alienation, but for severe cases, it is rarely sufficient and requires these types of court-ordered therapeutic interventions.

Biases in court. Given how complex parental alienation cases have become due to claims of abuse and neglect, judges have increasingly requested or required outside professionals to provide recommendations for how to assign custody.[20] Unfortunately, there are often maternal preferences for custody, even when mothers are found to be alienators. For example, Anna Lavadera and colleagues found evidence for maternal preference in a small qualitative review of Italian court cases in which parental alienation was occurring. Male alienators were treated differently than female alienators in that court experts *never* recommended they get custody. In contrast, court experts recommended that children remain in the custody of an alienating mother 40% of the time. Only when there are maternal deficits (e.g., mother has a mental illness, which may include substance abuse disorders) were fathers given custody.[21] All professionals involved with custody and high-conflict cases must be trained to understand how their biases about parental expectations and abilities influences their perceptions, and work towards minimizing the impact of these biases.

Misuse of domestic violence and parental alienation accusations. In several prior chapters, we discussed how a number of mothers and fathers have both made claims of either domestic violence or parental alienation occurring when, in fact, it was not. When false claims such as these are made, it undermines the intent of the original legislative policy (for domestic violence) and the legitimacy of the experience of parents who are *actually* alienated from their children. As a society, we need to discourage those who abuse the system in these ways, and we need to implement *reliable* strategies to differentiate between true and false claims for both types of accusations. We should not punish people simply for making accusations of parental alienation when there are objective criteria with which to evaluate its existence. Likewise, there should be a better mechanism to punish those who are found to make false accusations of domestic violence or abuse. For example, it is oftentimes illegal to report false claims of abuse to public service institutions like Child Protective Services, but false claims are rarely, if ever, punished. Courts need to enforce violations of the law and be responsive when a falsely accused parent requests intervention.

Legislative interventions

At the start of this book, we discussed the fact that many states across the U.S. and in other parts of the world have attempted to construct laws that make equal parenting time the default custodial recommendation. For example, legislators in Florida recently passed an equal parenting time law, only to have it stopped before it was signed into law. Many have blamed special interest groups such as child advocates for this obstruction. There have also been a number of ballot initiatives pushed in states such as North Dakota that have been beaten at the polls, their opponents being from the American Bar Association and child advocacy groups. The argument against these measures are that such a change would increase court costs and create a greater backlog of cases because child custody evaluations and determination processes are time consuming and expensive.[22]

This argument is weak because child custody evaluations are *already* time consuming and expensive. They are also currently standard practice in the vast majority of child custody disputes because they help the judge or magistrate determine what is in the "best interests of the child." If equal parenting time is the default way custody is assigned because it is considered to be in the child's best interest, then the subjectivity involved with this judicial determination is eliminated. *Children need both parents, and they should get equal time with them.* This change would eliminate a substantial number of child custody evaluations, and these would only then be ordered in cases where there is substantive evidence of one parent being possibly unable to parent effectively (e.g., police reports of abuse). The real reason for opposition to legislative and judicial change is the financial loss that such a change poses to professions that benefit from the status quo.

Indeed, litigation related to divorce has been estimated as a $28 billion industry,[23] and this does not include litigation related to drawn-out custody disputes, expert testimony fees, and other costs. Attorneys benefit from an adversarial court system, and often present one parent as warm and nurturing and the other as either aggressive or predatory.[23] In addition, there are many examples of corrupt relationships between judges, specific law firms, child custody evaluators, and other court professionals that rule in favor of the clients willing or able to pay the most money.[24] This is one of the reasons the State of Colorado has passed a law limiting the fee charged by Child Family Investigators (CFIs) to a maximum of $2,000.[25] Greater oversight of family court systems and professional conflicts of interest are needed, and much of this can be accomplished through judicial and legislative reforms.

Family court officials interpret and follow the law; many do so quite subjectively and indiscriminately. Changes to laws that set guidelines for resolving parental disputes, custody, and parental alienation are needed in order to make changes in how they are enforced. Unfortunately, there are many cases in which judicial systems have not cooperated with legislative branches to apply laws that are intended to serve in the best interests of children. For example, the state of Nebraska recently spent $150,000 to study a) what family courts do regarding child custody, and b) whether revisions to a Parenting Act made in 2007 that recommended more equal parenting time allocations resulted in better child outcomes after divorce. The only data that the researchers were able to gather indicated that even though there were rarely accusations of abuse, fathers in Nebraska were rarely granted custody (only 13.8% of the time), and were granted shared custody to an even lesser extent. The researchers were not able to get information on the well-being of the children, because the custody recommendations outlined in the act were not even being followed by the family court judges.[26]

We know that sanctions, fines, and other deterrents for law breaking work to some extent, but only if behaviors are monitored and deterrents are applied. Although people do not always obey the speed limit, they do comply when they know that their speed can be monitored and the law will be enforced. What would happen if there was no monitoring or ticketing for speeding? Would people start speeding more often? Most likely. Many of the parents we interviewed provided similar analogies. Although there may be clear court orders about parents having specific visitation times, there is no one appointed to monitor or enforce them. The alienator can obstruct all contact with minimal consequence.

Laws need to be created with the teeth to enforce them, otherwise these behaviors will just continue and increase over time. In 2014, Oklahoma was one of the first U. S. states to pass a law (Senate Bill 1612) that requires custodial parents to honor court-ordered visitation schedules or face punishment. The bill acknowledges that many non-custodial parents do not have the money to enforce their visitation rights and that custodial parents need to know that it is their *duty* to facilitate visits with the other parent. If they do not, then the non-custodial parent simply needs to fill out a form with the courthouse, much like small claims court, and the court would re-evaluate the visitation schedule or punish the violating parent with fines or jail time. It remains to be seen whether this approach will be effective at curbing violations of court-ordered parenting time, but it is an important step in the right direction.[27]

How can we stop parental alienation?

Children need both parents, as well as extended family and other loving people in their lives (e.g., step-parents, grandparents). Most of the research we have on parenting has been with mothers because *there is even a bias within psychology that mothers are just "better" at being parents than fathers.* Positive mothering behaviors and a secure attachment to the mother has been associated with healthy social, cognitive, and language development that has long-lasting effects across the child's life. Fewer studies have included fathers. We know less about their role in child development except within the context of the two-parent family. Psychological theories on attachment between parents and children have suggested that it is the sensitive, day-to-day interactions between parent and child that makes the child more securely attached to a parent. However, research indicates that this is truer for mothers than fathers. For fathers, a positive relationship with their child is driven by whether they have a positive relationship with the mother. The father's attachment to their child is not as directly related to how sensitive they are to the child's needs as it is to their relationship with their mother.

Despite what we know about how important both mothers and fathers are and how a positive relationship between both parents is important for a child's psychological health, there has still been a lot of resistance from the general public to changes in law that make equal parenting time between parents the standard. *Many still believe that children do not need both parents,* and this belief has also influenced legislators, judges, magistrates, mental health professionals, and other influential professionals who make decisions that affect families impacted by parental alienation.

Successfully addressing parental alienation will require attacking this problem from every angle. First, we all need to examine our own biases and stereotypes that we have about men and women in parental roles. Stereotypes about men and women, mothers and fathers are formed at a very young age (2 years old) and are very resistant to change. How do your beliefs about what it means to be a mother or father influence how you view other parents' behaviors? When you see a father at an airport traveling alone with a crying infant versus a mother doing the same thing, would you be likely to help one or the other more? If a father has to leave work early to pick up his children from school, do you evaluate him differently than a mother doing the same thing? If a mother complains about the father not caring for or not spending enough time with his children, are you more apt to believe that than if a father says the same thing about the mother? If a father tells you that his ex-wife refuses to let him see his children, would you assume that there must be a good reason for it? Would you make the same assumption if it was a mother not being able to see her children?

Our expectations and the stereotypes we have about parents greatly influence, consciously *and* automatically, how we assign blame in cases of parental alienation. In other words, it is our own biases, as insiders and outsiders that are perpetuating and exacerbating this problem. We are all to blame. *Our laws and policies are created by the very people who have biases and stereotypes about parental expectations.* After we become aware of our own biases, we next need to put a critical lens to how our rules and regulations regarding divorce and custody disputes perpetuate and even encourage this problem.

Parental alienation is something that happens within families, intact or broken, but it is not a private issue. Asking parents to just get along, or to "kiss and make up" in these cases shows a clear naiveté about what parental alienation is. In cases of parental alienation, one parent has more power and control over the other because of the children. *These parents take satisfaction in severing the relationship of their children with the other parent.* Bullies and their victims cannot just "work things out" by talking about their issues in a room together-- they need outside intervention because there are serious power differentials operating and strong motives on behalf of the bully to not get along. *Parental alienation is an adult form of bullying.* We cannot just stand by and watch parents bully each other. Bystanders such as extended family, neighbors, friends, schools, and the courts should not allow such bullying and relational aggression to occur, as our society's children are suffering.

The parental alienation problem is a social and cultural one. It impacts friends, extended family, schools, extra-curricular programs, financial institutions, employers, mental and physical health providers, and overburdened criminal and civil court systems. *Deniers and minimizers of parental alienation are supporters of the behavior, and those who stay silent are culpable as well.* It is time we see this problem from the systemic perspective it is, and how each and every one of us contributes to it in advertent and inadvertent ways. We hope that this book reframes this problem for you with a more nuanced understanding of how not only we, but our social and cultural systems have made this a difficult problem to fix. Interventions and solutions that are sensitive to the larger social context in which these troubled families live will be more effective than those that address only pieces of the puzzle. We need to do this for our children and generations that follow.

REFERENCES

Chapter 2

[1]Garber, B. D. (2011). Parental alienation and the dynamics of the enmeshed parent-child dyad: Adultification, parentification, and infantilization. *Family Court Review, 49,* 322-335.

[2]Wallerstein, J. E., & Kelley, J. B. (1976). The effects of parental divorce: Experiences of the child in later latency. *American Journal of Orthopsychiatry, 46,* 256-269.

[3]Gardner, R. A. (1998). Recommendations for dealing with parents who induce a parental alienation syndrome in their children. *Journal of Divorce & Remarriage,* 28(3/4), 1-21.

[4]Rand, D. C. (2011). Parental alienation critics and the politics of science. *The American Journal of Family Therapy, 39,* 48-71.

[5]Bernet, W. (2008). Parental alienation disorder and DSM-V. *American Journal of Family Therapy, 36,* 349–66.

[6]Bernet, W., von Boch-Galhou, W., Baker, A. L., & Morrison, S. L. (2010). Parental alienation, DMS-V, and ICD-11. *American Journal of Family Therapy, 38,* 76-187.

[7]Lavadera, A. L., Ferracuti, S., & Togliatti, M. M. (2012). Parental alienation syndrome in Italian legal arguments: An exploratory study. *International Journal of Law and Psychiatry, 35,* 334-342.

[8]Kelly, J. B., and Johnston, J. R. (2001). The alienated child: A reformulation of Parental Alienation Syndrome. *Family Court Review, 39,* 249-266.

[9]Johnston, J. R. (2003). Parental alignments and rejection: An empirical study of alienation in children of divorce. *Journal of the American Academy of Psychiatry and the Law, 31,* 158-170.

[10]Darnell, D. (2008). *Divorce Casualties: Understanding Parental Alienation.* New York, NY: Taylor Publishing Group.

[11]Vincent, L. (Feb. 8, 2003). Little girls lost? *WORLD magazine.* (Volume 18; Number 5)

http://www.worldmag.com/displayarticle.cfm?id=6825

[12]Fidler, B., & Bala, N. (2010). Children resisting postseparation contact with a parent: Concepts, controversies, and conundrums. *Family Court Review, 48*(1),

10-47.

Chapter 3
[1]Johnston, J. R. (2003). Parental alienation and rejection: An empirical study of alienation in children of divorce. *The Journal of the American Academy of Psychiatry and the Law, 31,* 158-170.
[2]Bruch, C. (2001). Parental alienation syndrome and parental alienation: Getting it wrong in child custody cases. *Family Law Quarterly, 35,* 527-552.
[3]Emery, R. E. (2005). Parental alienation syndrome: Proponents bear the burden of proof. *Family Court Review, 43,* 8-13.
[4]Viljoen, M., & van Rensburg, E. (2014). Exploring the lived experiences of psychologists working with parental alienation syndrome. *Journal of Divorce & Remarriage, 55,* 253-275.
[5]Lavadera, A. L., Ferracuti, S., & Togliatti, M. M. (2012). Parental alienation syndrome in Italian legal arguments: An exploratory study. *International Journal of Law and Psychiatry, 35,* 334-342.
[6]Baker, A. (2010). Adult recall of parental alienation in a community sample: Prevalence and associations with psychological maltreatment. *Journal of Divorce and Remarriage, 51,* 16-35.
[7]Clawar, S. S., & Rivlin, B. V. (1991). *Children held hostage: Dealing with programmed and brainwashed children.* Chicago, IL: American Bar Association.
[8]U.S. Census Bureau. (2009). Living arrangements of children. Retrieved on November 21, 2015 from https://www.census.gov/prod/2011pubs/p70-126.pdf
[9]Bernet, W. (2010). Parental Alienation DSM-5, and ICD-11. Springfield, Illinois: Charles C. Thomas Publisher, Ltd.
[10]Harman, J. J., Biringen, Z., Ratajack, E. R., Outland, P., & Krauss, A. (under review). Parents behaving badly and the sanctioning of them for doing so.
[11]Harman, J. J., Elder, S. L., & Biringen, Z. (in preparation). *Prevalence of parental alienation in a representative adult sample.*
[12]U. S. Census Bureau. (2015). State and County QuickFacts. Retrieved on November 23, 2015 from http://quickfacts.census.gov/qfd/states/00000.html
[13]Mone, J. & Biringen, Z. (2012). Perceived parental

alienation: Reliability and validity of a new instrument. *Divorce & Remarriage, 53,* 157-177.
[14]Bhattacherjee, A. (2012). Social Science Research: Principles, Methods, and Practices. *Textbooks Collection.* Book 3. http://scholarcommons.usf.edu/oa_textbooks/3
[15]Rueda, C. A. (2004). An inter-rater reliability study of Parental Alienation Syndrome. *The American Journal of Family Therapy, 32,* 391-403.
[16]Berry, D. B. (1995). *Domestic Violence Sourcebook.* Los Angeles, CA: Lowell House.
[17]Saini, M., Johnston, J. R., Fidler, B. J., & Bala, N. (2012). Empirical studies of alienation. In K. Kuehnle & L. Drozd (Eds.), *Parenting Plan Evaluations: Applied Research for the Family Court* (pp. 399-441). New York: Oxford University Press.

Chapter 4
[1]Garber, B. (2011). Parental alienation and the dynamics of the enmeshed parent-child dyad. *Family Court Review, 49,* 322-335.
[2]Darnall, D. (1998). *Divorce casualties: Protecting your children from parental alienation.* Dallas, TX: Taylor Publishing Company.
[3]Kelly, J. B., & Johnston, J. (2001). The alienated child: A reformulation of Parental Alienation Syndrome. *Family Court Review, 39,* 249-266.
[4]Lavadera, A. L., Ferracuti, S., & Togliatti, M. M. (2012). Parental alienation syndrome in Italian legal arguments: An exploratory study. *International Journal of Law and Psychiatry, 35,* 334-342.
[5]Johnston, J. R. (2003). Parental alienation and rejection: An empirical study of alienation in children of divorce. *The Journal of the American Academy of Psychiatry and the Law, 31,* 158-170.
[6]Lowenstein, L. F. (2010). Attachment theory and alienation. *Journal of Divorce & Remarriage, 51,* 157-168.
[7]Statistics South Africa (2011). *Marriages and divorces, 2010.* Pretoria, South Africa: Author.
[8]Bala, N., Hunt, S., & McCarney, C. (2010). Parental alienation: Canadian court cases 1989-2008. *Family Court Review, 48,* 164-179.
[9]Maccoby, E. E., & Mnookin, R. H. (1992). *Dividing the Child: Social and legal dilemmas of custody.* Cambridge, MA: Harvard

University Press.

[10]Carser, D. (1979). The defense mechanism of splitting: Developmental origins, effects on staff, recommendations for nursing care. *Journal of Psychiatric Nursing and Mental Health Services, 17*, 21–28.

[11]Bowlby, J. (1980). *Attachment and Loss*, Vol. 3: Loss, sadness and depression. New York: Basic Books.

[12]American Psychiatric Association. (2013). *Diagnostic and statistical manual of mental disorders* (5th ed.). Washington, DC: Author.

[13] Wakefield, H., & Underwager, R. (1990). Personality characteristics of parents making false accusations of sexual abuse in custody disputes. *Issues in Child Abuse Allegations, 2,* 121-136.

[14]National Institute of Mental Health. (n.d.) Borderline Personality Disorder. Retrieved on November 11, 2015 from http://www.nimh.nih.gov/health/topics/borderline-personality-disorder/index.shtml

[15]Zalewski, M., Stepp, S. D., Scott, L. N., Whalen, D. J., Beeney, J. F., Hipwell, A. E. (2014). Maternal borderline personality disorder symptoms and parenting of adolescent daughters. *Journal of Personality Disorders, 28,* 541-554.

[16]Crandell, L. E., & Hobson, R. P. (1999). Individual differences in young children's IQ: A social-developmental perspective. *Journal of Child Psychology and Psychiatry, 40,* 455-464.

[17]Crandell, L. E., Fitzgerald, H. E., & Whipple, E. E. (1997). Dyadic synchrony in parent-child interactions: A link with maternal representations of attachment relationships. *Infant Mental Health Journal, 18,* 247-264.

[18]Goodman, G., Bartlett, R. C., & Stroh, M. (2013). Mothers' borderline features and children's disorganized attachment representations as predictors of children's externalizing behavior. *Psychoanalytic Psychology, 30,* 16-36.

[19]Gunderson, J. G., & Lyoo, I. K. (1997). Family problems and relationships for adults with borderline personality disorder. *Harvard Review of Psychiatry, 4,* 272-278.

[20]Burgo, J. (2015). *The narcissist you know: Defending yourself against extreme narcissists in an all-about-me age.* New York: Touchstone.

[21]Blais, M.A., Smallwood, P., Groves, J.E., Rivas-Vazquez, R.A. (2008). Personality and personality disorders. In T.A. Stern, J. F. Rosenbaum, M. Fava, J. Biederman, & S. L., Rauch (Eds.), *Massachusetts General Hospital Clinical Psychiatry, 1st ed. (ch. 39). Philadelphia, PA: Mosby Elsevier.*

[22]Ehrenberg, M. F., Hunter, M. A., & Elterman, M. F. (1996). Shared parenting agreements after marital separation: The roles of empathy and narcissism. *Journal of Consulting and Clinical Psychology, 64*(4), 808-818.

[23]Trumpeter, N. N., Watson, P. J., O'Leary, B., J., & Weathington, B. L. (2008). Self-functioning and perceived parenting: Relations of parental empathy and love inconsistency with narcissism, depression, and self-esteem. *The Journal of Genetic Psychology: Research and Theory on Human Development, 169*(1), 51-71.

[24]Horton, R. S., Bleau, G., & Drwecki, B. (2006). Parenting narcissus: What are the links between parenting and narcissism? *Journal of Personality, 74*, 345-376.

[25]Golomb, M., Fava, M., Abraham, M., & Rosenbaum, J. F. (1995). Gender differences in personality disorders. *American Journal of Psychiatry, 152*, 579-582.

[26] Tschanz, B. T., Morf, C. C., & Turner, C. W. (1998). Gender differences in the structure of narcissism: A multi-sample analysis of Narcissistic Personality Disorder. *Sex Roles, 38*, 863-870.

[27]Baker, A. (2007). *Adult Children of Parental Alienation Syndrome: Breaking the Ties That Bind.* New York: W. W. Norton and Company, Inc.

[28]Trupe, R. D. (2013). The effect of maternal borderline personality disorder and social support on patterns of emotional availability in mother-child interactions, doctoral dissertation, The University of Tennessee, Knoxville.

[29]Landry, S. & Menna, R. (2006). *Early intervention with multi-risk families: An integrative approach.* Baltimore, MD: Paul H. Brookes Publishing.

[30]Garber, B. D. (2011). Parental alienation and the dynamics of the enmeshed parent-child dyad: Adultification, parentification, and infantilization. *Family Court Review, 49*, 322-335.

[31]Eysenck, M.W. (2004). *Psychology: An international perspective.*

New York, NY: Psychology Press Inc.

[32]Easterbrooks, M.A., Biesecker, G., & Lyons-Ruth, K. (2000). Infancy predictors of emotional availability in middle childhood: the roles of attachment security and maternal depressive symptomatology. *Attachment & Human Development, 2,* 170-187.

[33]Giancarlo, C., & Rottman, K. (2015). Kids come last: The effect of family law involvement in parental alienation. *The International Journal of Interdisciplinary Social Sciences: Annual Review, 9,* 27-42.

[34]Viljoen, M., & van Rensburg, E. (2014). Exploring the lived experiences of psychologists working with parental alienation syndrome. *Journal of Divorce & Remarriage, 55,* 253-275.

Chapter 5

[1]Gith. E. (2013). The attitude of the Shari'a courts to parental alienation syndrome: Understanding the dynamics of the syndrome in Arab society. *Journal of Divorce & Remarriage, 54,* 537-549.

[2]Ceci, S. J., & Bruck, M. (1999). *Jeopardy in the courtroom: A scientific analysis of court testimony.* Washington, DC: American Psychological Association.

[3]Loftus, E. F. (1997). Creating false memories. *Scientific American, 277,* 70-75.

[4]Mone, J. & Biringen, Z. (2012). Perceived parental alienation: Reliability and validity of a new instrument. *Divorce & Remarriage, 53, 157-177.*

Chapter 6

[1]Johnston, J. R., & Roseby, V. (1997). *In the Name of the Child: A Developmental Approach to Understanding and Helping Children of Conflicted and Violent Divorce.* New York: Free Press.

[2]Eysenck, M.W. (2004). *Psychology: An International Perspective.* New York, NY: Psychology Press Inc.

[3]Festinger, L. (1957). *A Theory of Cognitive Dissonance.* Stanford, CA: Stanford University Press.

[4]Johnston, J. R. (2003). Parental alienation and rejection: An empirical study of alienation in children of divorce. *The Journal of the American Academy of Psychiatry and the Law, 31,* 158-170.

[5]Werner, S. (2009). *Understanding the effects of child sexual abuse,*

New York: Routledge.
[6]de Fabrique, N., Romano, S. J., Vecchi, G. M., & van Hasselt, V. B. (2007, July). Understanding Stockholm Syndrome. *FBI Law Enforcement Bulletin (Law Enforcement Communication Unit)* 76(7), 10–15.
[7]Boulet, T. R., & Anderson, S. M. (1986). 'Mind control' and the battering of women. *Cultic Studies Journal, 3*, 25-35.
[8]Van IJzendoorn, M. H. (1995). Adult attachment representations, parental responsiveness, and infant attachment. A meta-analysis on the predictive validity of the Adult Attachment Interview. *Psychological Bulletin, 117*, 387-403.
[9]Sorce, J. F., Emde, R. N., & Frank, M. (1982). Maternal referencing in normal and Down's syndrome infants: A longitudinal analysis. In R.N. Emde & R.J. Harmon (Eds.) *The development of attachment and affiliative systems* (pp. 281-292), New York: Plenum.
[9]Macfie J., Fitzpatrick, K. L., Rivas, E. M., & Cox, M. J. (2008). Independent influences upon mother-toddler role reversal: Infant-mother attachment disorganization and role reversal in mother's childhood. *Attachment & Human Development, 10*(1), 29–39.
[10]Mone, J. & Biringen, Z. (2012). Perceived parental alienation: Reliability and validity of a new instrument. *Divorce & Remarriage, 53, 157-177.*
[11]Gith. E. (2013). The attitude of the Shari'a courts to parental alienation syndrome: Understanding the dynamics of the syndrome in Arab society. *Journal of Divorce & Remarriage, 54,* 537-549.
[12]Lowenstein, L. F. (2013). Is the concept of parental alienation a meaningful one? *Journal of Divorce & Remarriage, 54,* 658-667.
[13]Pagani, L. S., Japel, C., Vaillancourt, T., & Tremblay, R. E. (2010). Links between middle-childhood trajectories of family dysfunction and indirect aggression. *Journal of Interpersonal Violence, 25(*12), 2175-2198.
[11]Peris, T. S., Goeke-Morey, M. C., Cummings, E. M., & Emery, R. E. (2008). Marital conflict and support seeking by parents in adolescence: Empirical support for the parentification construct. *Journal of Family Psychology, 22,* 633-

642.

[12]Jacobvitz, D., Hazen, N., Curran, M., & Hitchens, K. (2004). Observations of early triadic family interactions: Boundary disturbances in the family predict symptoms of depression, anxiety, and attention-deficit/hyperactivity disorder in middle childhood. *Development & Psychopathology, 16*, 577-592.

[13] Garber, B. D. (2011). Parental alienation and the dynamics of the enmeshed parent-child dyad: Adultification, parentification, and infantilization. *Family Court Review, 49*, 322-335.

[14]Stirling, J. (2007). Beyond Munchausen Syndrome by Proxy: Identification and treatment in child abuse in medical setting. *Pediatrics, 119*, 1026-1030.

[15]Daehnert, C. (1998). The False Self as a means of disidentification: A psychoanalytic case study. *Contemporary Psychoanalysis, 34*, 251-271.

[16]Baker, A. J. L., & Darnall, D. C. (2007). A construct study of the eight symptoms of severe parental alienation syndrome: A survey of parental experiences. *Journal of Divorce & Remarriage, 47*, 55-75.

Chapter 7

[1]Bala, N., Hunt, S., & McCarney, C. (2010). Parental alienation: Canadian court cases 1989-2008. *Family Court Review, 48*, 164-179.

[2]Vassilou, D., & Cartwright, G. F. (2001). The lost parent's perspective on parental alienation syndrome. *American Journal of Family Therapy, 29*, 181-191.

[3]Giancarlo, C., & Rottman, K. (2015). Kids come last: The effect of family law involvement in parental alienation. *The International Journal of Interdisciplinary Social Sciences: Annual Review, 9*, 27-42

[4]Baker, A. J. L. (2010). Even when you win you lose: Targeted parents' perceptions of their attorneys. *The American Journal of Family Therapy, 38*, 292-309.

[5]Kelly, J. B., & Johnston, J. (2001). The alienated child: A reformulation of Parental Alienation Syndrome. *Family Court Review, 39*, 249-266.

[6]Johnston, J. R. (2003). Parental alienation and rejection: An

empirical study of alienation in children of divorce. *The Journal of the American Academy of Psychiatry and the Law, 31,* 158-170.

[7]Braver, S. L., Griffin, W., Cookston, J. T., Sandler, I. N., & Williams, J. (2005). Promoting better fathering among divorced non-resident fathers. In W. M. Pinsof & J. L. Lebow (Eds.), *Family Psychology: The Art of the Science,* pp. 295-325. New York: Oxford University Press.

[8]Kruk, E. (2010). Collateral damage: The lived experiences of divorce mothers without custody. *Journal of Divorce & Remarriage, 51,* 526-543.

[9]Gardner, R. A. (1989). *Family evaluation in child custody, mediation, arbitration, and litigation.* Cresskill, NJ: Creative Therapeutics.

[10]Bureau of Justice Statistics. (2015). Data collection: Court Statistics Project. Retrieved from http://www.bjs.gov/index.cfm?ty=dcdetail&iid=283

[11]Viljoen, M., & van Rensburg, E. (2014). Exploring the lived experiences of psychologists working with parental alienation syndrome. *Journal of Divorce & Remarriage, 55,* 253-275.

Chapter 8

[1]Eibl-Eibesfeldt, I. (1989). *Human ethology.* New York: Aldine de Gruyter. (Chapter 4 on Social Behavior).

[2]Sidanius, J., & Pratto, F. (1999). *Social Dominance.* Cambridge, United Kingdom: Cambridge University Press.

[3]Walby, S. (2001). Theorising patriarchy. In M. Waters (Eds.), *Critical Concepts: Volume II, Cultural Modernity.* London: Routledge.

[4]Wall, J. C. & Amadio, C. (1994). An integrated approach to child custody evaluation: utilizing "best interests" of the child and family system frameworks. *Journal of Divorce and Remarriage, 21,* 39-57.

[5]Lowenstein, L. F. (2013). Is the concept of parental alienation a meaningful one? *Journal of Divorce & Remarriage, 54,* 658-667.

[6]Pleck, J. H. (1998). American fathering in historical perspective. In K. V. Hansen & A. I. Garey (Eds.), *Families in the U.S.: Kinship and Domestic Politics,* pp. 351-361.

Philadelphia, PA: Temple University Press.

[7]Thurer, S. (1995). *Myths of motherhood: How culture invents the good mother.* New York: Penguin Books.

[8]Grisso, T. (1986). *Evaluating competencies: Forensic instruments.* New York: Plenum Press.

[9]Chapin, H. (1974). Cat's in the cradle. On *Verities & Balderdash.* Bridgeport Connecticut: Elektra. (1973).

[10]Bly, R. (1990). *Iron John: A Book about Men.* Boston, MA: Addison-Wesley Publishing Company, Inc.

[11]Flood, M. (2012). Separated fathers and the 'father's rights' movement. *Journal of Family Studies, 18,* 235-245.

[12]Livingston, G. (2014, June). Growing number of dads home with the kids: Biggest increase among those caring for family." Washington, D.C.: Pew Research Center's Social and Demographic Trends project.

[13] Luftman, V. H., Veltkamp, L. J., Clark, J. J., Lannacone, S., & Snooks, H. (2005). Practice guidelines in child custody evaluations for licensed clinical social workers. *Clinical Social Work Journal, 33,* 327-357.

[14]Viljoen, M., & van Rensburg, E. (2014). Exploring the lived experiences of psychologists working with parental alienation syndrome. *Journal of Divorce & Remarriage, 55,* 253-275.

[15]French, J., & Raven, B. (1959). The bases of social power. In D. Cartwright (Ed.), Studies in social power (pp. 150–167). Ann Arbor, MI: Institute for Social Research.

[16]Simpson, J. A., Farrell, A. K., Oriña, M. M., & Rothman, A. J. (2015). Power and social influence in relationships. In M. Mikulincer, P. R. Shaver, J. A. Simpson, & J. F. Dovidio (Eds.), *APA Handbook of Personality and Social Psychology, Vol. 3: Interpersonal Relations* (pp. 393-420). Washington, DC: American Psychological Association.

[17]Pratto, F. Lee, I., Tan, J. Y., & Pitpitan, E. V. (2011). Power basis theory: A psychoecological approach to power. In D. Dunning (Ed.), *Social Motivation,* pp. 191-222. New York: Psychology Press.

[18]Pleck, J. H. (1998). American fathering in historical perspective. In K. V. Hansen & A. I. Garey (Eds.), *Families in the U.S.: Kinship and Domestic Politics,* pp. 351-361. Philadelphia, PA: Temple University Press.

[19]Ickes, W. E. (1997). *Empathetic accuracy*. New York: The Guilford Press.

[20]Rudman, L. E., & Phelan, J. E. (2008). Backlash effects for disconfirming gender stereotypes in organizations. *Research in Organizational Behavior, 28*, 61-79.

[21]American Association of University Women (2015). The simple truth about the gender pay gap. Retrieved on July 8, 2015 from http://www.aauw.org/resource/the-simple-truth-about-the-gender-pay-gap/

[22]Prentice, D. A., & Carranza, E. (2002). What women should be, shouldn't be, are allowed to be, and don't have to be: The contents of prescriptive stereotypes. *Psychology of Women Quarterly, 26*, 269-281.

Chapter 9

[1]Tjaden, P., & Thoennes, N. (2000). U.S. Dep't of Just., NCJ 183781, *Full Report of the Prevalence, Incidence, and Consequences of Intimate Partner Violence Against Women: Findings from the National Violence Against Women Survey, at iv* (2000), available at http://www.ojp.usdoj.gov/nij/pubs-sum/183781.htm

[2]Archer, J. (2000). Sex differences in aggression between heterosexual partners: A meta-analytic review. *Psychological Bulletin, 126*, 651-680.

[3]Whitehouse.gov (n.d.) Factsheet: Violence against women Act. Retrieved on October 21, 2015 from www.whitehouse.gov/.../default/files/docs/vawa_factsheet.pdf

[4]U.S. Government Publishing Office. (2013). The Violence Against Women Act (2013). Retrieved on July 7, 2015 from http://www.gpo.gov/fdsys/pkg/BILLS-113s47enr/pdf/BILLS-113s47enr.pdf.

[5]Schulte, K. E. (2014). Restoring balance to abuse cases: Expanding the one-sided approach to teaching domestic violence practice. *Columbia Journal of Gender and the Law, 28*, 1-54.

[6]Stop abusive and violent environments (2010). Domestic violence programs discriminate against male victims. Retrieved on July 7, 2015 from http://www.saveservices.org/reports/

[7]Bettencourt, A. B., & Miller, N. (1996) Gender differences

in aggression as a function of provocation: A meta-analysis. *Psychological Bulletin, 119,* 422-447

[8]Goldshield, J. (2015). *Gender Neutrality and the "Violence Against Women" Frame,* 5 U. Miami Race & Soc. Just. L. Rev. 307   Available   at: http://repository.law.miami.edu/umrsjlr/vol5/iss2/9

[9]Saunders, D. G. (2015). Research based recommendations for child custody evaluation practices and policies in cases of intimate partner violence. *Journal of Child Custody, 12,* 71-92.

[10]Giancarlo, C., & Rottman, K. (2015). Kids come last: The effect of family law involvement in parental alienation. *The International Journal of Interdisciplinary Social Sciences: Annual Review, 9,* 27-42.

[11]Collins, E. R. (September 2, 2014). The evidentiary rules of engagement in the war against domestic violence. 90 New York University Law Review, May 2015, Forthcoming. Available at SSRN: http://ssrn.com/abstract=2490698

[12]Bow, J. N., Gould, J. W., & Flens, J. R. (2009). Examining parental alienation in child custody cases: A survey of mental health and legal professionals. *The American Journal of Family Therapy, 37,* 127-145.

[13]Rand, D. C. (2011). Parental alienation critics and the politics of science. *The American Journal of Family Therapy, 39,* 48-71.

[14]Heim, S., Grieco, H., Di Paola, S., & Allen, R. (2002). *Now Family Court Report.* Available from Califormia National Organization for Women, 926 "J" St., Ste. 424, Sacramento, CA 94814, www.canow.org.

[15]Ceci, S. J., & Bruck, M. (1999). *Jeopardy in the courtroom: A scientific analysis of court testimony.* Washington, DC: American Psychological Association.

[16]Saunders, D. G. (2015). Research based recommendations for child custody evaluation practices and policies in cases of intimate partner violence. *Journal of Child Custody, 12,* 71-92.

[17]Schulte, K. E. (2014). Restoring balance to abuse cases: Expanding the one-sided approach to teaching domestic violence practice. *Columbia Journal of Gender and the Law, 28,* 1-54.

[18]Clemente, M., & Padilla-Racero, D. (2015). Are children susceptible to manipulation? The best interest of the

children and their testimony. *Children and Youth Services Review, 51*, 101-107.

[19]Raven, B. H. (1964). *Social influence and Power.* Los Angeles, CA: Ft. Belvoir Defense Technical Information Center

[20]Bernet, W., Verrocchio, M. C., & Korosi, S. (2015). Yes, children are susceptible to manipulation: Commentary on article by Clemente & Padilla-Pacero. *Children and Youth Services Review, 56*, 135-138.

[21]Flood, M. (2012). Separated fathers and the 'father's rights' movement. *Journal of Family Studies, 18*, 235-245.

[22]Twenge, J. M., Konrath, S., Foster, J. D., Campbell, W. K., & Bushman, B. J. (2008). Egos inflating over time: A cross-temporal meta-analysis of the narcissistic Personality Inventory. *Journal of Personality, 76*(4), 875-902.

[23]Burgo, J. (2015). The narcissist you know: Defending yourself against extreme narcissists in an all-about-me age. New York: Touchstone.

[24]Holtzworth-Munroe, A. (2005). Female perpetuation of physical aggression against an intimate partner: A controversial new topic of study. *Violence and Victims, 20*, 251-259.

[25]Nelson, D. A., Springer, M. M., Nelson, L. J., & Bean, N. H. (2008). Normative beliefs regarding aggression in emerging adulthood. *Social Development, 17*, 638-660.

[26]Arnocky, S., Sunderani, S., Miller, J. L., & Vaillancourt, T. (2012). Jealousy mediate the relationship between attractiveness comparison and females' indirect aggression. *Personal Relationships, 19*(2), 290-303.

[27]Cameron, E. Z., Linklater, W. L., Stafford, K. J., & Minot, E. O. (2003). Social grouping and maternal behaviour in feral horses (Equus caballus): the influence of males on maternal protectiveness. *Behavioral Ecology and Sociobiology, 53*, 92-101.

[28]Sterk, E. H. M., Watts, D. P., & van Schaik, C. P. (1997). The evolution of female social relationships in nonhuman primates. *Behavioral Ecology and Sociobiology, 41*, 291-309.

Chapter 10

[1]Pleck, J. H. (1998). American fathering in historical perspective. In K. V. Hansen & A. I. Garey (Eds.), *Families in the U.S.: Kinship and Domestic Politics*, pp. 351-361.

Philadelphia, PA: Temple University Press.

[46]Schoppe-Sullivan, S. J., Altenburger, L. E., Settle, T. A., Kamp Dush, C. M., Sullivan, J. M., & Bower, D. J. (2015). Expectant fathers' intuitive parenting: Associations with parent characteristics and postpartum positive engagement. *Infant Mental Health Journal, 35,* 409-421.

[3]Hand, K. (2006). Mothers' accounts of work and family decision-making in couple families. *Family Matters 75,* 70-76.

[4]Giancarlo, C., & Rottman, K. (2015). Kids come last: The effect of family law involvement in parental alienation. *The International Journal of Interdisciplinary Social Sciences: Annual Review, 9,* 27-42.

[5]Rothbart, M., & Taylor, M. (1992). Category labels and social reality: Do we view social categories as natural kinds? In G. R. Semin (Ed.), *Language, Interaction, and Social Cognition,* pp. 11-36. Thousand Oaks, CA: Sage Publications, Inc.

[6]Okimoto, T. J., & Heilman, M. E. (2012). The 'pad parent' assumption: How gender stereotypes affect reactions to working mothers. *Journal of Social Issues, 68,* 702-724.

[7]Walzer, A. S., & Czopp, A. M. (2011). Mother knows best so mother fails most: Benevolent stereotypes and the punishment of parenting mistakes. *Current Research in Social Psychology, 16,* ArtID: 12

[8]Perera, D. N., Short, L., & Fernbacher, S. (2014). There is a lot to it: Being a mother and living with a mental illness. *Advances in Mental Health, 12,* 167-181.

[9]Orthwein, J. (2010). Filicide: Gender bias in defense attorneys' perception of motive and defense strategies. Dissertation abstracts international: Section B: the Sciences and Engineering. Vol 71 (3-B), p. 2095.

[10]Yourstone, J., Lindholm, T., Grann, M., & Svenson, O. (2008). Evidence of gender bias in legal insanity evaluations: A case vignette study of clinicians, judges, and students. *Nordic Journal of Psychiatry, 62,* 273-278.

[11]Rüsch, N., Angermeyer, M. C., & Corrigan, P. W. (2005). Mental illness stigma: Concepts, consequences, and initiatives to reduce stigma. *European Psychiatry, 20,* 529-539.

Chapter 11

[1]Siegal, J. C., & Langford, J. S. (1998). MMPI-2 validity scales

and suspected parental alienation syndrome. *American Journal of Forensic Psychology, 16,* 5-14.

[2]Lavadera, A. L., Ferracuti, S., & Togliatti, M. M. (2012). Parental alienation syndrome in Italian legal arguments: An exploratory study. *International Journal of Law and Psychiatry, 35,* 334-342.

[3]Viljoen, M., & van Rensburg, E. (2014). Exploring the lived experiences of psychologists working with parental alienation syndrome. *Journal of Divorce & Remarriage, 55,* 253-275.

[4]Garber, B. D. (2011). Parental alienation and the dynamics of the enmeshed parent-child dyad: Adultification, parentification, and infantilization. *Family Court Review, 49,* 322-335.

[5]Toren, P., Bregman, B. L., Zohar-Reich, E., Ben-Amitay, G., Wolmer, L., & Laor, N. (2013). Sixteen-session group treatment for children and adolescents with parental alienation and their parents. *The American Journal of Family Therapy, 41,* 187-197.

[6]Baker, A. (2012). Resisting the pressure to choose between parents; A school-based program. *International Cultic Studies Association, 3, 8-13.*

[7]Bala, N., Hunt, S., & McCarney, C. (2010). Parental alienation: Canadian court cases 1989-2008. *Family Court Review, 48,* 164-179.

[8]Lowenstein, L. F. (2013). Is the concept of parental alienation a meaningful one? *Journal of Divorce & Remarriage, 54,* 658-667.

[9]Giancarlo, C., & Rottman, K. (2015). Kids come last: The effect of family law involvement in parental alienation. *The International Journal of Interdisciplinary Social Sciences: Annual Review, 9,* 27-42.

[10]Lowenstein, L. F. (2011). What if the custodial parent refuses to cooperate with child contact decisions? *Journal f Divorce & Remarriage, 52,* 322-325.

[11]Herbst, D. (2015, July 10). Michigan judge releases kids she jailed for refusing to visit father. Retrieved on September 27, 2015 from http://www.people.com/article/michigan-judge-sends-kids-jail-refusing-estranged-father.

[12]Baker, A. J. L. (2010). Even when you win you lose:

Targeted parents' perceptions of their attorneys. *The American Journal of Family Therapy, 38,* 292-309.
[13]Gith. E. (2013). The attitude of the Shari'a courts to parental alienation syndrome: Understanding the dynamics of the syndrome in Arab society. *Journal of Divorce & Remarriage, 54,* 537-549.
[14]Fidler, B. and Bala, N. (2010). Children resisting postseparation contact with a parent: Concepts, controversies, and conundrums. *Family Court Review, 48*(1), 10-47.
[15]Warshak, R. (2010). "Family Bridges: Using insights from social science to reconnect parents and alienated children." *Family Court Review, 48* (1), 48-80.
[16]Reay, K. (2015). Family Reflections: A promising therapeutic program designed to treat severely alienated children and their family system. *American Journal of Family Therapy, 43,* 197-207.
[17]Sullivan, M.J. et al. (2010). "Overcoming Barriers Family Camp." Family Court Review, *48* (1), 116-135.
[18] Friedlander, S. & Walters, M.G. (2010). When a child rejects a parent: Tailoring the intervention to fit the problem. *Family Court Review, 48* (1), 98-111.
[19]Ellis, E.M. (2005). Support for the alienated parent. *American Journal of Family Therapy, 33,* 415-426.
[20]Mnookin, R. H. (1975). Child custody adjudication: Judicial functional in the face of interdeterminancy. *Law and Contemporary Problems, 39,* 226-292.
[21]Lavadera, A. L., Ferracuti, S., & Togliatti, M. M. (2012). Parental alienation syndrome in Italian legal arguments: An exploratory study. *International Journal of Law and Psychiatry, 35,* 334-342.
[22]Houchin, T. M., Ranseen, J., Hash, P. A., & Barnicki, D. J. (2012). The parental alienation debate belongs in the courtroom, not in DSM-5. *The Journal of the American Academy of Psychiatry and the Law, 40,* 127-131.
[23]Hoffman, L. (2006, November 6). To have and hold onto. Forbes.com.   Retrieved   from http://www.forbes.com/2006/11/07/divorce-costs-legal-biz-cx_lh_1107legaldivorce.html on July 6, 2015.
[24]Bow, J. N., Gould, J. W., & Flens, J. R. (2009). Examining

parental alienation in child custody cases: A survey of mental health and legal professionals. *The American Journal of Family Therapy, 37,* 127-145.

[25]Supreme Court of Colorado (2011, April). Directive concerning court appointments of child and family investigators pursuant to C. R. S. 14-10-116.5. Office of the Chief Justice, Chief Justice Directive 04-08.

[26]Franklin, R. (2015, November 16). Nebraska family court judges: Thwarting the will of the legislature? Retrieved on November 24, 2015 from https://nationalparentsorganization.org/blog/22673-nebraska-family-court-judges-thwarting-the-will-of-the-legislature

[27]Deaton, D. (June 3, 2014.) Noncustodial parent visitation rights bill signed into law. Retrieved on October 2, 2015 from http://okwnews.com/news/whatzup/whatzup-politics/104907-noncustodial-parent-visitation-rights-bill-signed-into-law.html

ABOUT THE AUTHORS

Jennifer J. Harman, PhD. is an Associate Professor of Psychology at Colorado State University and is the Program Coordinator for the Applied Social & Health Psychology Program. She is an accomplished and awarded teacher, and has published many peer-reviewed articles and textbooks on intimate relationships, such as The Science of Relationships: Answers to your Questions about Dating, Marriage and Family. She is also a contributor to ScienceofRelationships.com, a relationship science resource for the on-line community, and is interviewed as a relationship expert for many national and international media outlets (Chicago Tribune, the Denver Post, NY Magazine, datingadvice.com, and the Irish Independent). She was motivated to write this book and apply her expertise in social psychology to better understand and find solutions for parental alienation because she has been a target of it herself.

Zeynep Biringen, PhD is a Professor in the Department of Human Development & Family Studies at Colorado State University. She is an award-winning mentor and researcher and has published peer-reviewed research in the areas of parent-child relationships (attachment, emotional availability) in intact as well as divorced families. She has also developed prevention programs to enhance parent-child and teacher-child relationships. She developed the Emotional Availability (EA) Scales which have now been used in all U.S. subcultures, as well as at least 25 countries around the world, and is now becoming popular in relation to understanding mother-child as well as father-child emotional availability in custody and child protection evaluations. She has contributed to popular magazines (*Parenting, Prevention*), and has been interviewed for television (Court TV) and radio. Her concern in parental alienation issues is the children: She believes parental alienation is a spectrum problem and that even subtle and insidious cases of such hostility can negatively impact children.

Both authors are available for interviews and public speaking engagements. For inquiries, please email parentsactingbadly@gmail.com

Interested in getting more information about the book, the authors, examples of parental alienation cases (prototypes), or resources on the topic? Please visit our website at ParentsActingBadly.com

Made in the USA
Lexington, KY
21 July 2016